Praise for
You've Got to Be Kidding!

"I'm a parent of six. At times it seemed impossible! But nineteen? Incredible! Yet through such an enormous responsibility comes life lessons for us all. Wow! I mean, oh my!"

—DICK ENBERG, sports broadcaster

"This is the most wonderful guide for raising happy, healthy, self-confident children ever written! It will transform you, your children, and your home."

—BRIAN TRACY, motivational speaker and best-selling author

"*You've Got to Be Kidding!* is down to earth, full of biblical wisdom, and touches all the bases! Parents are in for a great read and will be greatly helped in raising their kids for God."

—JIM CYMBALA, pastor, Brooklyn Tabernacle Church

"This is more than a book—let's call it an incredible guide for living, whether you're a parent or not. Thank you, Pat and Ruth, for setting this high standard for all of us."

—CHRIS SCHENKEL, Hall of Fame sportscaster

"Pat and Ruth Williams are real and relevant as they share the delightful pleasures and the painful realities of raising nineteen children from various cultures within their own blended family. With the application of God's Word and prayer, they have magnificently and responsibly accepted all the challenges. Their story will enrich your own efforts through the marathons of life."

—CYNTHIA SWINDOLL, president and CEO, *Insight for Living*

You've Got to Be Kidding!

You've
Got to Be
Kidding!

Real-life parenting advice from a mom and dad of nineteen

Pat & Ruth
Williams

WaterBrook
Press

YOU'VE GOT TO BE KIDDING!
PUBLISHED BY WATERBROOK PRESS
2375 Telstar Drive, Suite 160
Colorado Springs, CO 80920
A division of Random House, Inc.

Details in some anecdotes and stories have been changed to protect the identities of the persons involved.

ISBN 9781578567034

Library of Congress Cataloging-in-Publication Data

Williams, Pat, 1940–
    You've got to be kidding! / Pat and Ruth Williams.— 1st ed.
        p. cm.
    ISBN-13: 978-1-578-56703-4
    1. Parenting—Religious aspects—Christianity. I. Williams, Ruth (Ruth E.) II. Title.
    BV4529.W575 2004
    248.8'45—dc22

                                                                                    2003027713

2004—First Edition

146635165

CONTENTS

ACKNOWLEDGMENTS

Ruth and I would like to acknowledge the support, guidance, and patience of the following people who helped make this book possible:

Special thanks go to Bob Vander Weide and John Weisbrod of the Orlando Magic family for allowing Pat the time to write his books. We are both so grateful.

We owe deep gratitude to Pat's assistant, Diana Basch, for all she does for our family and us.

We would like to give a huge salute to four dependable associates—proofreader Ken Hussar; Hank Martens, formerly of the Orlando Magic mail/copy room; our ace-typist Fran Thomas; and former intern Doug Grassian.

We owe a special debt of gratitude to Macario ("Angel") Garcia, our friend and house manager, who has made untold contributions to our family over the years. Angel, we couldn't have done it without you.

A hearty thanks is also due to Bruce Nygren and the wonderful staff at WaterBrook Press. Thank you for believing that we had something important to say and for providing the support and the forum to say it.

To our cohort in writing this book, Dave Wimbish: Thanks for your time, dedication, and perseverance. We got it done. Good job!

And, finally, special thanks and appreciation to our children. Whether they know it or not, each one of them contributed something very important to this book. They are truly the backbone of our lives and give us the inspiration to live each day to the fullest.

INTRODUCTION

No—we're not kidding! We have nineteen children.

That's right. Nineteen.

You should see mouths fall open and pupils dilate when we drop that bombshell on unsuspecting new acquaintances.

It happens every so often at a dinner party or other social gathering where we've just met someone for the first time. After we've chatted about the weather, the Orlando Magic's latest game, our jobs, or current events, the conversation almost always gets around to children.

"So…how many children do you have?"

We try to be as nonchalant as possible.

"Nineteen."

"Pardon me? I don't think I got that."

"I said nineteen."

"You've got to be kidding!"

Pat will often add, "I have parented nonstop, day-by-day, for thirty-two straight years and gone to Little League baseball games for twenty-one years without a single year off!"

At this point in the conversation, we've experienced a number of interesting reactions. Some people slap their ear with the palm of their hand as if there must be something wrong with their hearing. Others have sprayed us with a mouthful of whatever they happened to be drinking at the moment. But most people just say something like: "Good heavens! Why?"

The best answer we can give is, *This is what God wanted for us.*

"You're joking…right?"

Nope! Having nineteen children is no laughing matter.

"Did you *plan* on having nineteen kids?"

Of course not. Nobody would plan on having that many children!

"Are you two crazy?"

Crazy, no. Stressed and frazzled sometimes, you bet. Someone has said that having three or more children is like having a bowling alley in your brain. You can just imagine what things are like in *our* brains!

This is when the challenge comes: "What are your children's names?"

The person who asks this question always has a look on his or her face that says, "I bet you can't do it." But we can—and usually without even stopping to try to remember whom we've left out!

There are Jimmy, Bobby, Karyn and Stephanie, Sarah, Andrea and Michael, Thomas, Stephen and David. Then there's Peter, Brian, Sammy, Gabriela and Katarina, followed by Daniela, Richard, Caroline and Alan. That's a final score—so far—of eleven boys and eight girls!

At this point, after our new acquaintance's initial shock has worn off, we're always asked, "What's it like?"

Well, it ain't the Brady Bunch!

It's wild, it's crazy, it's frenetic, it's a never-ending stream of soccer, swim meets, tennis, volleyball, football, cheerleading, basketball, church youth groups, homework, skinned knees, broken hearts, carpools, runny noses, trips to the dentist, doctor visits, braces, parent-teacher conferences, and… Well, you get the picture.

With nineteen kids, we celebrate lots of birthdays. (Seven in the month of July alone.) And with all nineteen of our kids growing rapidly, we've had to shop for clothes about as often as most families shop for groceries. Thank goodness Ruth works for the FranklinCovey organization, where she spends a lot of her time teaching and coaching business executives how to get their lives organized. We have called upon every bit of her expertise to keep things running smoothly in the Williams household.

Still, having nineteen kids around the house means that every day is a college-level course in parenting. The things we've learned about parenting could fill a book—and this is the book!

Are we qualified to write such a book? Well...

- We know what it takes to parent children who are born to you.
- We know about raising adopted kids, including girls and boys from other cultures and ethnicities.
- We know the particulars of raising stepkids and dealing with the special problems that arise from trying to blend families.
- We even know what it's like to be a single parent.

We know all of this from direct personal experience: Pat has fathered four children, welcomed another fourteen kids into his family through adoption, and gained another daughter through his marriage to Ruth in 1997.

Ruth spent years as a single mother. Then, through marriage to Pat, she jumped feetfirst into his "family circus"—despite the incredulous reaction of some friends who warned her, "You'd better take some time to think about what you're getting yourself into." After doing what her friends suggested, she decided that the poet was right and that love would indeed conquer all. She married Pat, became a mother to an additional eighteen children of various ages, and has never looked back.

Now, having nineteen kids is no day at the beach. In other words, it's not easy. Ours is not a "television-family," where everything is tied up in neat little packages at the end of every episode. A couple of years ago, we had sixteen teenagers all at once. Can you imagine what it would be like to live in a house with teenage hormones bouncing off the floors, walls, and ceiling? It was like living in the middle of a hurricane!

Raising these children to be respectable, responsible adults has been the hardest thing either one of us has ever had to do. When you've parented nineteen kids, you've seen it all—every conceivable problem and pitfall of every age group, from the tiniest infant in her cradle to the much-taller-than-you young man heading off to find his own way in the world. But at the risk of sounding trite, we have to tell you that it has also been the most rewarding experience of our lives.

Every Child Is a Miracle

The Bible says in Psalm 127:3, "Behold, children are a gift of the Lord" (NASB). And so they are, even though that may be hard to remember when the school principal calls you for the third time in two weeks and asks, "Can you come in for a conference? We need to talk—*again!*"

Because you're reading this book, we're assuming that you, too, know the joys and pains associated with parenting. If so, think back to the first time you saw that little girl or boy who is "bone of your bone and flesh of your flesh." Or think back to when the person at the orphanage placed that little hand in yours and said, "You can take him home now. He's all yours." Like us, you probably dreamed about what that tiny little guy would become when he grew up.

Like most parents, you have made plans for the new arrival; sacrificed your own needs and wants; saved money (or tried to) for things like college and weddings even though they may seem to be as far into the future as *Star Trek*. As parents, we teach, we laugh, we cry—and we get down on our knees and pray, pray, pray that we do and say things the right way so that our precious little bundle will grow up to be a happy, contributing, successful, and independent human being.

Sometimes our children actually live up to our dreams and expectations. And, sadly, sometimes they don't. As parents, we have experienced the ultimate highs with the children who do it right and the devastating lows with the children who don't.

The things we've learned in the trenches are distilled into this book. But we'd be misleading you if we tried to tell you this is an "advice book." If there is one thing that stands out in what we have learned over the years, it is this: There are no simple answers. Just as no two snowflakes or sets of fingerprints are alike, no two children are alike. Just when you think you have heard, seen, and learned it all, something entirely new and unexpected happens—sometimes wonderful and sometimes awful.

Bottom line: We can't tell you what you should do in any particular situation because every child and every situation is unique. However, we can pass on the benefit of our hard-earned wisdom learned from our own five or six lifetimes' worth of parenting. We have made mistakes. There are some things we would go back and do differently, but that's impossible. So we simply keep going, ask for God's guidance, and do our best every day. More than anything else, we want this book to encourage you to keep investing your time, energy, and love into your children—even in that daughter who seems to be beyond your reach and beyond hope, and even when that son has long since grown up and flown from the nest. You see, parenting is a lifelong commitment. And despite all the confusion, frustration, conflict, heartbreak, and loud music, the words of the psalmist are still true. Children really are an inheritance from the Lord! And yes, that includes teenage children.

PART ONE

The Beginning

Chapter 1

HOW IT ALL BEGAN

B efore we move on to what we've learned during our time together, let us take a couple of moments to answer the question that's on your mind. Namely, how did we get nineteen children? We'd better let Pat tell that story:

At thirty-two, I was a young hotshot sports executive working as general manager of the Chicago Bulls long before Michael Jordan first came into the league. The Bulls weren't very good when I arrived in 1969—just as they weren't very good after Michael left. But I was determined to bring the Windy City a winning basketball team—and I did. We made the NBA play-offs each of the four seasons I was with the team, and we threw a scare into some of the league's best teams.

I didn't have much of a social life, as I had devoted myself to building my career, and I had been very successful. When my (now) ex-wife began pursuing me, I was flattered—and eleven months later we were married.

Looking back on it now, I can see that my decision was much too hasty. We had dated briefly and had not really spent much time together. But she was very persistent and, as I said, I was flattered. Had we spent more time together, we would have discovered that we had very little in common. I loved sports; it was my chosen career. She didn't care about sports and loved music. It was not a good mix. We tried our best, but our marriage was difficult from the beginning, kind of like living in the shadow of a volcano.

But my career blossomed. From Chicago I went to Atlanta, where I served as general manager of the Hawks, and then back north to Philadelphia, where I moved to the front office of the 76ers and helped lead the team to the NBA championship in 1983.

Jimmy, Bobby, and Karyn were born during the first six years of our marriage, but my wife frequently talked about her desire to adopt children from another country. I listened—halfheartedly at best—and hoped it was just a phase that would pass.

It wasn't.

As our tenth wedding anniversary approached in 1982, her desire to adopt was so intense that the marriage would collapse if I didn't comply. I really wasn't sold on the idea, but I wanted to save the marriage. After discussions with several adoptive families, we discovered that South Korea had more children available for adoption than any other country in the world. And that's how it all began.

In September 1983, through Holt Children's Services in Eugene, Oregon, came two little girls—sisters, two and three years old, Sarah and Andrea. It was love at first sight, and it was a wonderful experience.

A year later Michael was born.

In 1986 we moved to Orlando, where I headed an effort to bring a professional basketball team to central Florida. In 1987 the Holt people contacted us about two boys, five-year-old twins from South Korea. Thomas and Stephen joined the family shortly before their sixth birthdays. Now there were eight children—and I was hooked! There were so many children who needed help. If I could, I would have adopted all of them!

So I was ready to listen when the adoption agency called to tell us about four boys in Mindanao, the southernmost island of the Philippines. These little guys had spent weeks living on the street before they'd finally been taken to an orphanage. After I heard their story, I said to the Holt people, "Well, send some pictures." They did, and it started a wrestling match with my wife. She felt we had enough children, but I was relentless. I felt that God was pushing me to go after these four boys. And so eleven-year-old David became a Williams, along with Peter, ten, Brian, nine, and little Sammy, who was six.

Now there were twelve children at home, and I loved it. We were adding bedrooms, hiring a cook, employing a full-time nanny—doing everything we could to stay on top of the situation.

Then came the fall of Romania.

When that country's communist regime toppled in 1989, the world discovered that over a million boys and girls were wasting away in state-owned orphanages after being abandoned by parents who simply couldn't afford to care for them. It broke my heart to see news reports from Romania, where children were growing up in run-down warehouselike conditions, totally deprived of human love and comfort. I felt I had to do something. And so Gabriela and Katarina, both age five, came to live with us in 1991. This time, my wife was thrilled.

Now there were fourteen.

But this wasn't the end.

When we went on vacation to Brazil in the summer of 1992, Daniela and Richard were added to the clan, and while picking them up, I met two more children: Caroline, ten, and Alan, eight, a brother-and-sister combination. I asked, "What's going to become of them?" The social worker told us that Caroline would probably wind up as a teenage prostitute and that Alan probably wouldn't live to see his eighteenth birthday.

I couldn't let that happen. "We've got to get them out of here," I said.

And so, on Christmas night of 1993, Caroline and Alan arrived at Orlando International Airport. Television cameras were on hand to record the scene for a halftime report during the NBA's Christmas night game. For me it was a joy. But no matter how many children we added to the household, my wife was not happy.

A month later she moved all of her belongings into our guesthouse and announced that she was going to look for a house of her own. She no longer wanted to be married to me. Of course I was shocked and, for a time, devastated.

For the next year and a half, she contemplated the new direction she wanted her life to take. The kids stayed with me, and I became a single parent to eighteen.

Yes, I had a lot of hired help. I had a full-time staff consisting of a cook, a driver, a nanny, and a housekeeper. But when it came to being the dad—

providing a sympathetic listening ear when it was needed, imposing discipline when it was required, attending parent-teacher conferences, helping with homework, and, in short, doing all the things that parents normally do—I was the one. I was also running a basketball team, which took a lot more than forty hours a week. Beyond that, I was out on the lecture circuit, writing books, and doing what I could to keep up with my household expenses. Even though I'm an up-tempo kind of guy with plenty of natural energy, there were weeks when I was completely exhausted and trying to get by on very little sleep.

During most of this time, I lived with the hope that my marriage would somehow be saved. But as the weeks passed, it became increasingly clear that wasn't going to happen. In late December 1995 my wife finally filed for divorce.

A NEW BEGINNING

It took another year for the divorce to move through the courts. It was bitter and unpleasant and emotionally draining. I lost most of my money and other assets, but I was able to keep the kids with me. I knew I could always make more money, but I wasn't willing to leave my kids.

It was during this emotionally trying time that God surprised me with joy and brought an unexpected treasure into my life.

Her name was Ruth.

Ruth first had a tremendous influence upon me as a mentor and coach. (I'll let her explain that.) As that relationship grew, she became a trusted and much-appreciated friend.

Friendship deepened into love, and I became aware that I would always regret it if I let her get away. It is quite impossible for me to tell you what Ruth means to me, but she basically saved my bacon.

Within two years she brought my dismal financial situation back to life, and she made our nearly empty, drab house bright and cheerful and filled it with love. She became the companion and partner I had never had and, very importantly, became the caring, loving mother my children needed. She completely changed my life for the better.

I (Ruth) knew the moment I met him that Pat was a charming, articulate, and attractive gentleman.

I didn't know he had eighteen children.

Had I known, I might not have spent an hour standing and talking to him in a parking lot on a very hot, very steamy afternoon.

When I first met Pat, I thought my parenting days were just about behind me. My own daughter, Stephanie, had grown into a beautiful, poised, and confident young woman. She had graduated from the University of Florida in sports management and was beginning her career as a sports executive with the Tampa Bay Storm, an Arena Football team. (As you can imagine, she and Pat hit it off immediately!)

I had been single for five years. Although I had become entrenched in my speaking and training career, I had always thought that I'd like to remarry and have another child—perhaps even two! I prayed every night that God would send a Christian man into my life. I wanted that more than anything, but God hadn't seen fit to do that—yet.

As time went by and my career began demanding more and more of my time and attention, I had gradually given up on romance. If I couldn't have Mr. Right, I would rather stay single, and I had gotten pretty used to that idea. In fact, I said to God one night, "Okay, God, I get the message. I give up."

I suppose in some ways I regretted the fact that Stephanie had never had any little brothers or sisters to play with, but we had always been close, and I was proud of the adult she was becoming. She made me feel that I'd done a good job as a parent. Little did I know what was ahead.

I first met Pat when I was conducting a time-management seminar for the Orlando Magic staff. My presentation was scheduled for the final three hours of a two-day staff retreat. The weather was brutally hot, and I didn't find out until much later that Pat had initially been displeased about having to come to my presentation. He was tired and just wanted to go home.

As for me, I wasn't even supposed to be in Orlando that day. In fact, I had a previous engagement. But Kelly Wallace, the woman who put the retreat together for the Magic, had attended one of my seminars a few months earlier, and she insisted that I be the one to speak to the Magic staff.

As it turned out, the only place they could fit me in was during the last three hours, a time when a lot of folks check their watches and think about the things they have to do when they get home.

Pat figured that I was going to bore him to sleep.

Obviously, that's not what happened.

As soon as the seminar concluded, Pat was one of the first who came forward to tell me how much he had enjoyed it. He even stayed around to help me pack things up, and then he offered to help me carry everything out to my car. That's where it all started. As I mentioned earlier, we stood talking for nearly an hour in the parking lot under the broiling sun.

As we discussed the time-management techniques I'd presented, I was certain that my makeup was melting—and so was I. I was wearing a new, rather expensive business suit, which wasn't exactly ideal for the 95-degree temperature and 100 percent humidity of a late summer day in Florida.

Pat was extremely enthusiastic about the techniques I had presented because, until that time, he had been making notes on the backs of envelopes to try to keep track of his entire life. Despite Pat's obvious sense of humor and his enthusiasm for the FranklinCovey program, I could tell that something was wrong. There was something in his eyes that wasn't quite right. I didn't know that I was seeing the pain of a very difficult divorce.

He asked for my business card (which is now framed and hanging on the wall in his office), and we stayed in touch over the next few weeks through voicemail and phone calls, first as colleagues, then as friends. It was many months later before our relationship turned in a different direction.

In one of our get-to-know-each-other conversations, Pat asked if I had any regrets about my life. I said, "Not really. But I wish I had had more children."

He looked like he was going to laugh out loud, but he restrained himself and said, "I think I can fix that. I just may be the man for you."

As it turned out, he was so right.

When I met the children, it was love at first sight: I loved them and they loved me. In fact, months later, Pat's daughter Karyn said to her father, "Dad, we'd like Ruth for our stepmother. She's awesome!" That sealed the deal.

Pat officially proposed to me in February 1997, about eighteen months after our first meeting. In fact, he took me back to the same spot in the same parking lot where we had had our first chat, presented me with a beautiful ring, and in a poem he had written, asked me to marry him. We were married that April in the backyard of Pat's longtime friend and mentor, Jay Strack.

We chose a passage from the book of Ruth in the Bible and adjusted it slightly. In addition to loving, honoring, and submitting to each other for the rest of our lives, we also said the following: "Where you go I will go, and where you stay, I will stay. Your people shall be my people and your God my God; and"—I turned and looked at the children as I made the next promise—"your children shall be my children." And so our children were present for the start of our wonderful life of adventure together.

Was I prepared? I thought so. But how could anybody be prepared to become a mom to not one, but to nineteen children?!

I do not come from a big family. It was just my brother and me, growing up in an upper-middle-class Louisiana family. I was fortunate to be raised in a loving, Christian home. Our adopted children did not have that opportunity. In fact, none of them knew Jesus until Pat began taking them to church and explaining to them how much God loved them.

So, in some ways, I was not at all prepared for this new assignment, even though I have a master's degree in psychology and was working on my Ph.D. in organizational behavior and development. But I'm a quick learner, and I've discovered that it is possible to "win" as a parent no matter how many children you have. It just takes a lot of love, hard work, time, and attention.

And it takes the right mate.

God sent me the right one. I call Pat my "Renaissance Jock." He's quite a paradox. He is a true jock: driven, motivated, hard-working, dedicated, and determined. But he's also loving and warm and funny and kind. Our story has been a true fairy tale for me. You see, no matter how hectic it gets with the kids and our two careers, Pat takes time for me. Since our wedding on April 5, 1997, there hasn't been a day that I don't get anywhere from two to five messages from Pat telling me how much he loves me, how proud he is of me, how wonderful I am, or how thankful he is for me. He doesn't enter or leave a room without kissing me or hugging me or touching me in some way.

He even sings to me and recites poetry to me. (The kids think he's lost it when he does this, but I love it.) He brings me flowers and leaves me cards all over the house. In fact, whenever I go out of town and open my suitcase at the hotel—I'm still not sure when or how he does this—I always find a funny or mushy card telling me how much he misses me and that he can't wait for me to get home.

Pat makes sure we have a date at least once a week at minimum. He cuts a fresh grapefruit for me every morning when I'm home. He constantly brings me articles and books that he thinks might help in my business presentations. Without a doubt, he is the most considerate, loving man I've ever known. He puts the same energy, dedication, and determination into our marriage that he does into his speaking, writing, and sports.

We talk about everything and laugh a lot. We both do public speaking and love Broadway, sports, and running. We have finished twelve marathons together. We truly are best friends.

We have built our dream marriage, and at the same time, we have the joy of seeing our children grow and launch their own lives. I can only hope that they each find what we have.

When people ask us, "Are you going to adopt any more kids?" we laugh and say no. We're waiting for grandchildren—and we've calculated that we could wind up with sixty or more. It will certainly be another interesting chapter in our lives.

But back to raising nineteen children. What's it really like? Let me start off by giving you some recent snapshots from the days of our lives:

- One Thursday evening I returned from a speaking engagement in

Miami. Pat had left that day for an out-of-town speech. Once again, he and I were running full speed in opposite directions.

Almost as soon as I walked in the house, the phone rang. It was one of our teenage daughters who had left home before finishing high school. She had not been living the way she knew she should, and she wanted a chance to start over.

She admitted that she had nowhere to go and wanted to move into our guesthouse for a couple of months to try to get her life back on track. (The following Monday she moved in.)

• On Friday morning Caroline came to me as I was getting dressed, took both my hands in hers, looked at me with tears almost breaking the surface, and said, "Mother, I have to talk to you about Dimitry. [Dimitry was her fiancé of about three months.] It's really important, but I can't do it now or I'll start crying. I have to go to work. Could we have dinner—just the two of us—later tonight? Please!"

Meanwhile Kati had an eye appointment at 11:00 a.m. She had been having headaches and felt pressure behind her eyes. We spent two hours waiting and going in and out of the doctor's office for different tests. The conclusion was that Kati needed glasses for reading, so we ordered them.

Upon returning home I had a message from Caroline asking where we could meet and wanting to know, "Would it be possible for Dad to be there?"

I could not imagine what she wanted to talk about. Many possibilities whirled around in my mind. Pat was out of town, so I went alone. It turned out that Dimitry was possibly being sent to Japan for five years, and she wanted to get married before he left so she could go with him.

• On Saturday Pat returned from his trip, and we sat down with Caroline to discuss the responsibilities of marriage. Fortunately, her fiancé's deployment was changed to California. On October 10, 2003, Caroline became Mrs. Dimitry Givans.

While we were tackling the marriage discussions, our oldest daughter, Stephanie, came into town and asked me to help her find a new condo. She had just gotten a new job with Player Management Group and moved from Tampa to Orlando. So…we spent the rest of Saturday looking at condos with the second oldest daughter, Karyn, who had just recently gotten her real estate license. This would be her first sale—kind of neat that her sister was her first client.

The bottom line of all this is that in two days we welcomed home a returning prodigal, got glasses for Kati, became heavily involved in marriage discussions, and spent hours searching for a condo. It was a whirlwind! But almost every week has days like this. It comes with the territory when you have nineteen children. Our life can be hectic, but it is oh-so-rewarding!

If I ever wondered whether becoming a mother of nineteen was worth it, my fears were wiped away by this note from Sarah: "I just wanted to thank you for everything. I knew the first time I saw you, you and Daddy were meant for each other forever. Thank you for marrying him and loving us kids as your own. Love, Sarah."

In the pages ahead we're going to share some of the blessings of parenting—as well as some of the burdens—we've experienced while raising nineteen children. Sometimes those blessings are admittedly a little hard to find. But if we look deep, we can always find them, even in the most difficult situations.

The life we lead is not for the faint of heart. You have to be brave to raise nineteen kids. But these days you have to be brave to raise one kid! The journey of parenting is scary, but it can be the greatest, most rewarding adventure you'll ever have.

Are you ready?

Come on! Let's go.

PART TWO

The Blessings and Burdens
of a Full House

Chapter 2

EVERY CHILD IS UNIQUE

*There never were in the world
two opinions alike, no more than
two hairs or two grains; the most
universal quality is diversity.*
MICHEL DE MONTAIGNE

The best way to describe dinner in the Williams household is to say that it resembles a meeting of the General Assembly of the United Nations. The outward differences between our children are easy to see. Some are light skinned and light eyed; others have dark brown skin, hair, and eyes. Some are Hispanic, others are of Asian origin, and still others are Caucasian.

One quick glance will tell you that our kids come from different parts of the world. But there are other, deeper, differences that are harder to see. Some of our children are gifted athletes. Others are inclined toward music or art. Some have sailed through school without ever spending much time in study, while others have worked very hard to maintain a C average. Some have dropped out of high school, and others have earned their master's degree. Some of our children are introspective, by nature quiet and thoughtful. Others are like the Energizer Bunny and very vocal.

In other words, every child is different, so every child requires unique parenting. For example, each child presents different discipline issues and requires different discipline methods. One time Alan was grounded at home for getting a detention at school. One of our rules is that when you get in trouble at school, you also get grounded at home. We want our kids to be respectful and follow the school rules. So when Alan got the detention, we took away his PlayStation 2 for a week. When we did this, he asked, "Why don't you ground me from the phone like you do Caroline?" We responded, "Alan, you never use the phone. That wouldn't be punishment for you. It is for Caroline because she spends a lot of time on the phone." Other kids might lose their driver's license or television privileges. The punishment may be different, but our children are treated equally and fairly.

In addition, what motivates one child does not motivate another. We can't expect all of our kids to excel in the same areas of life. Yet we can, and do, expect each child to follow our family rules and guidelines. We expect all of our children to give their best effort at whatever they do. If we can help them do that, we're happy.

In his junior year of high school, Alan was named captain of the basketball team, and we were delighted to know that the effort he put forth on the court had paid off. We knew that he had given it his very best effort. But we also knew that he'd made a good effort when he came home with anything higher than a C in English class. For Alan to get a grade less than an A does not mean that he didn't try his best. But if his sister came home with a D in English, we'd know she didn't try very hard; she's capable of doing better.

Sometimes it's hard to accept and appreciate differences in children. Human nature being what it is, we naturally favor children who want to follow in our footsteps or who have the same dreams and aspirations for themselves that we have for them. It's also natural to be hurt or disappointed when our children don't share our same strengths in life or when they have no interest in or aptitude for things we feel passionate about. All this is natural…but it's wrong just the same.

WHEN LIFE IMITATES ART

Perhaps you saw the movie *Billy Elliot*. Poor Billy. His father wanted him to be a "macho" guy, a boxing champion, but all Billy wanted to do was dance. He was good at it too—naturally gifted, you might say. But his father didn't want him to be a "sissy." Now how would you feel if Billy Elliot were your son? Or how would you feel if you wanted your little girl to be a cheerleader, but she was more interested in playing on the football team? Every child is unique. Every child is blessed with certain abilities and desires. And it's our job, as parents, to help our children discover and fulfill their individual, God-given abilities.

Perhaps the *Billy Elliot* story is an extreme example. Usually the difference between what parents want for their children and what children want for themselves is not so obvious. We know, for instance, parents who have always put a high priority on education. They both have doctorates. He's an M.D.; she's a college professor. In high school and again in college, they both graduated near the top of their respective classes.

They were shocked when one of their sons, Adam, struggled in school. They accused him of not trying. They brought in tutors to help him. They grounded him for bad grades. They tried everything. Nothing they did could get Adam's grades higher than a C average.

But if you gave that boy a couple of pieces of wood and some tools, he could build you just about anything you wanted. And we're not talking about ordinary furniture either. He made beautiful, elegant chests and tables, with intricate patterns worked into them. He was an artist, but his parents didn't see it that way.

Adam's older sisters and brother had gone to prestigious universities, and his parents just assumed he would follow in their footsteps. He didn't want to go to college, but he didn't want to go against his parents' wishes either. So, even though Adam didn't have the best of grades, his mom and dad managed to pull a few strings and get him into a top school in the Midwest. They hoped that he was just a late bloomer who would catch on sooner or later. But that didn't happen.

Adam almost made it through two semesters before he decided that this just wasn't what he wanted to do with his life. He decided that he was going to drop out of school and pursue a career in carpentry.

That was nearly ten years ago now. Looking back on it, Adam is certain that he made the right decision. He makes a comfortable living (even if his income isn't big enough to suit his dad). He finds satisfaction in what he does. Other people know him as a fine craftsman.

He is on relatively good terms with his parents, but notes, with sadness, that he can still sense they are disappointed that he didn't become a psychologist, like his brother, or an attorney, like his sister. (Perhaps Adam's folks have forgotten that Jesus Christ was also a carpenter, a trade he learned from his father, Joseph.)

Our point is that children in the same family can be very different from one another—amazingly so. That's not surprising when you think of all the thousands of different genetic combinations that can go into one child's makeup. Therefore, we feel that one of our tasks as parents is to help our children find and develop the strengths that are unique in each of them. Imagine how boring the world would be if we were all skilled in the same area. What if we were *all* artists or athletes or singers or writers or rocket scientists? Besides, it seems to us that we most deeply admire people who can do things that we can't do. For example, our daughter Karyn sings beautifully, but Pat doesn't have the world's best singing voice. That's why he has such tremendous respect and admiration for singers like The Three Tenors. But if we could all sing like they do, we wouldn't appreciate their talent nearly as much.

Think how boring the world would be if we all liked the same music, the same food, the same movies, the same everything! Diversity makes the world a better, more exciting place. Once we become comfortable with diversity, we realize it's a *good thing.* That's true in the world at large, and it's true in families, too.

The Williams family has discovered that there is true beauty and joy in diversity. Here are four important things we've learned (sometimes the hard way) about celebrating—not just tolerating—differences.

1. Don't Compare Children to One Another
We have learned from experience that there is absolutely no value in comparing our children to one another in terms of grades, behavior, obedience, or any other area of life. We have made the mistake of doing that to our kids once in

a while, and they always hate it. So we try not to make negative comparisons such as:

- "Why can't you get A's in math, like your brother does?"
- "Just look at how well your sister is behaving. Why can't you be more like her?"
- "Another note from your teacher about acting up in class? Your sister has never brought home a single note from any of her teachers."
- "We've never had this kind of trouble with any of your brothers or sisters."

Such comments may be intended to motivate, but they almost always have the opposite effect. The child who hears such things can instead be demoralized by the fact that she does not measure up to her siblings in her parents' eyes. She may feel resentful and angry toward her brothers and sisters who've made her look bad. Instead of being challenged by her siblings' accomplishments, she may simply give up, thinking, "Oh, what's the use? I can never be as good as they are anyway."

We try not to compare our children in "positive" ways either. This means we don't say things like:

- "Wow! Look at your sister's report card. Straight A's! I want to see you do that next semester."
- "Did you see the game your brother had yesterday? Four hits in five at-bats. But I bet you'll do even better than that in your game tomorrow."
- "You're a faster swimmer than your sister was at your age. I can't wait to see what you're going to do in high school!"

We feel, based on personal experience, that such statements put undue pressure on children to meet their parents' expectations. We have seen that making comparisons between children is always counterproductive.

2. Don't Push Your Expectations on Your Children

Now, despite what we just said, there *are* certain things we expect from all of our kids.

- We expect them to try hard.
- We expect them to be honest.
- We expect them to be good citizens (courteous, polite, trustworthy, and so on).
- We expect them to stay away from drugs and alcohol while they're living under our roof.
- We expect them to attend church and Sunday school.
- We expect them to show respect for us and to obey the rules we have established.

Within that context they are free to do what they feel like doing. We don't push any particular sport or activity, but we don't expect our children to sit around and do nothing. We want them to be involved in activities that will help them develop into well-rounded individuals. But instead of trying to get them to do what *we* want them to do, we urge them to think about what *they* want to do, and then we help them do it.

It's good to let children choose their path.

Some parents drag their young daughters to auditions and acting lessons or push them to participate in beauty pageants. These parents may think they are doing it for their child's benefit, but most of the time they're only living out their own desires and fooling themselves. It is a huge mistake for any parent to try to live his dreams through his children.

Your kids should be living their own dreams—not yours. When parents try to force *their* dreams on their children, it doesn't work. Many times children feel rejected by parents who do this. They may feel as if they're not okay. And they may ultimately turn to other people to find the love and acceptance they need from their parents.

It means so much to children to have their parents' acceptance and approval.

Our friend Bruce was absolutely beside himself when his son Henry, a gifted athlete, decided to quit playing football after his freshman year in college. Henry decided to quit the sport even though his coach told him he was almost assured of starting at cornerback his sophomore year. Bruce begged

Henry not to "blow this opportunity." He reminded his son (one more time) about how his own promising career had been cut short by a knee injury and how he would have given just about anything to be back out there on the gridiron.

"I know, Dad," Henry apologized. "I've always enjoyed playing football, but I just don't love it the way you do." He explained that he was more interested in pursuing his studies than in playing cornerback.

"But you've always loved football," Bruce protested. He reminded his son of all his accomplishments in Pop Warner, junior high, and high school. All those trophies he'd won. All those posters, jerseys, and other football memorabilia that cluttered the walls of his bedroom.

Henry shook his head. "Dad," he said quietly, "I did all that more for you than for me."

Fortunately Bruce heard what his son was saying, backed off, and let Henry make up his own mind about things. It wasn't easy, especially at first, but he finally got used to the idea of not being the father of a football player.

As for Henry, today, seven years later, he has his degree and is on his way to a successful career in business. Does he regret quitting the football team?

"The only thing I regret is that I know it hurt my dad's feelings," he says.

It is true that, as Johann Wolfgang von Goethe said, "We can't form our children on our own concepts; we must take them and love them as God gives them to us."

Before we move on to the next point, we'd like to answer a question we've been asked lots of times: "Do you think parents should stay completely out of it when it comes to guiding their children onto a particular path for their life?"

There's such a fine line between guiding and letting children choose and pushing them and choosing for them. Even when we can see that they may be making a mistake, all we can do is offer our opinion. The ultimate decision is theirs. Recently we experienced this with Caroline.

All during high school she talked about going to cosmetology school. She wanted to do hair, and she practiced on all her friends. In her junior year she got a job as an assistant at the salon where I (Ruth) get my hair done.

Everyone loved her. They constantly bragged about her abilities and were thrilled that she would one day be working with them as a stylist.

Then suddenly Caroline decided that she wanted to go into nursing. She's not that good in science or math, and she gets weak at the sight of blood. But out of the blue, she wanted to be an LPN (Licensed Practical Nurse).

We discussed it at length.

"Why?" we asked.

"I want to learn something new, do something different," she answered.

We explained that practical nurses make less money, work longer hours, and do a lot of "grunt" work that hair stylists don't do.

"I'll be fine," she said. "Money isn't that important." (I laughed to myself when I heard that!)

In this instance, though, there was no dissuading her. Her mind was made up, so we finally said, "Okay, it's your life."

She did not do well on the entrance test the first time. Her response was that she would take it as many times as necessary to pass it and get into nursing school. She passed the second time.

We certainly have to give her credit for tenacity and perseverance. It will be interesting to see how it all turns out. We would choose hair; she is choosing nursing.

Ultimately, it is her choice and we will support her.

What it all really comes down to is a matter of motive. All of us want to help our children discover and act upon their strengths and passions in life. The book of Proverbs talks about the importance of helping children stay on the path that's right for them: "Train a child in the way he should go, and when he is old he will not turn from it" (Proverbs 22:6). Boy! Do we ever hang on to this scripture a lot! To us, this verse means to train children in character and discipline and then let them apply the principles in whatever area of life they choose.

We have seen some parents push their child to do something that would make them feel happy and fulfilled instead of helping her find a path in life that will make *her* happy and fulfilled. If your dreams for your child coincide with her dreams for herself, so much the better! If not, support your children in their choices and pray for their success.

Author/pastor David Jeremiah comments on the verse from Proverbs we just mentioned:

> Each child needs to know that he is unique and not like any other
> child God every created. The Hebrew phrase, "in the way," describes
> the habit or character of an individual at his own age level. The empha-
> sis is on the importance of adjusting our training according to the abil-
> ity of the child at each stage of his development. Each child has his own
> way, and by paying attention, we can determine what that way is.

We believe that it's absolutely necessary to give our children the benefit of our wisdom and experience, but we know that's not always easy to do. Your children will always need your advice. But they will also need your blessing to be who God meant them to be.

3. Treat Each Child Like a Guest in Your Home

Never forget that children are not a possession. You do not "own" your sons and daughters. They are individual human beings whom God has entrusted to your care until they are wise enough and strong enough to make it on their own.

Keeping this in mind, we have always tried to treat our children as if they were guests in our home. No, that doesn't mean that we we treat them with cold formality. It does mean that we strive to be on our best behavior at all times. We say "please" when we want them to do something for us and "thank you" when they do it. We say "excuse me" if we accidentally bump into one of them. In other words, we treat them as if they are worthy of our respect—because they are!

It saddens us to hear the way some parents speak to their children in pub-lic places. They sound angry. They snap orders without the slightest show of respect. They use insulting words and abusive language. Nobody—especially defenseless children—should be treated that way.

If you had guests in your home, you'd want them to feel comfortable, secure, and welcome. You'd also want them to see you at your very best, not at your worst. That's what we mean when we say, "Treat your children as if they are guests!"

4. Don't Focus Your Attention on the "Stars"

"Mom always liked you best!"

Have you ever heard that? Have you ever said it? The Smothers Brothers built an entire career on such sibling rivalry, taking a subject that most of us find painful and turning it into hilarious comedy.

In the movie comedy *Mother,* Albert Brooks plays a forty-something writer who moves back in with his widowed mother (played superbly by Debbie Reynolds). He does this basically because he wants to try to figure out why she always liked his brother best. Even though this is an excellent movie, and very funny at times, it can also be difficult to watch because it hits so close to home for many people.

The truth is that—as Tom Smothers says and as Albert Brooks showed in his movie—even though parents may deny it, many of them do have favorite children Usually, the favorites are the ones who are cuter than the others, good-natured, polite, neat, athletic, obedient, helpful, content to play alone when there are no other kids around, and smarter than the others.

We've also seen tests suggesting that schoolteachers decide, very early in the year, which students are going to do well in class, and then they grade accordingly. A child who seems sloppy, a little disorganized, or different in some way just isn't going to get the same breaks as the child who sits politely at her desk, hands folded in front of her, listening intently to everything the teacher says.

Really, it's just human nature to feel better about children who are easy on the nerves. But we believe it's important for parents to make up their minds that, no matter what happens, they will not show favoritism toward any of their children—even those who are shining stars.

Our son-in-law Dale has been teaching kindergarten for five years. During the 2002–2003 school year, he had four students who stood out for their academic and social development. Dale says, "Connor, Taylor, Chase, and Kayla had good manners, great personalities, and were academically above average right from the beginning." He set out to learn what their parents had done to speed their children's development.

He discovered, first of all, that none of the children had ever been to day care. Connor's and Chase's moms stayed home with them until they reached school age. Kayla's and Taylor's moms returned to work soon after they were born, but both girls were cared for by their grandmothers.

Another common characteristic was that they were put into social situations at an early age. Taylor and Connor were expected to interact with other kids and their families. At eighteen months, Chase and Kayla were put into play groups for the purpose of developing their social skills.

All four of the children's mothers revealed that they read to their children on a daily basis. Kayla's mother, Shelly, said she read to Kayla and played music for her while she was still in the womb. Interestingly enough, Kayla seemed to recognize the same music after she was born. Chase's mom said she often read to him while he was lying in his crib. Even though she said she felt silly about it on occasion, she was also sure it would make a difference in his development.

Dale says, "As a kindergarten teacher, one of the things I look for at the beginning of the year is whether a child can hold a conversation with an adult and express himself appropriately. All four of these students do this exceptionally well. When I asked the parents how they spoke to their kids when they were younger, all four of them quickly pointed out that there was no baby talk in their households. They all talked to their kids in a normal fashion. Chase's mom told me that when her son was just learning how to talk, she would always tell him to enunciate his words. She was having a conversation with one of her friends one day when Chase walked up to her and reminded her, 'Mom, don't forget to e-nun-ci-ate.'"

The moral of the story? Believe in your kids. Author Kahlil Gibran wrote, "Children are living arrows that the parents send into the world." Expect great things from them. You might be surprised what they can do!

Chapter 3

SOME GET IT, SOME DON'T

Now then, my sons, listen to me;
blessed are those who keep my ways.
Listen to my instruction and be wise;
do not ignore it.
PROVERBS 8:32-33

P sychiatrist Ross Campbell says that three out of four children are "anti-authority" from the moment they're born, and from what we've seen, we'd certainly have to say that the man knows what he's talking about. Dr. Campbell says antiauthority children are the ones who come into the world "wanting to move your rules aside."

We have eight of those. We've had several who actually dropped out of high school—and each of our antiauthority children moved out of the house because they did not like our rules. They didn't want a curfew in high school. They felt they should be able to come in anytime they pleased. They didn't feel they should have to tell us where they were going or whom they were going with, and they didn't think they needed to study and make their grades. In other words, they didn't want to follow our basic family rules.

All our children were taught that these things are important. They had good role models. They were even rewarded for doing well in these areas. For example, children who followed the curfew rules, made their grades, and were good citizens at home were given cars when they got their driver's licenses. We let them buy the clothes they wanted. They could go out with their friends. However, any children who decided to leave home because they didn't want to follow the rules had to give up their cars. They were able to leave with their clothes and nothing else. If they wanted to be on their own, that was the way it was going to be. We expected them to get a job and support themselves.

Realize that we had many conversations with them about their decision to leave home before we felt they were really ready; we prayed fervently that God would reveal their mistake to them. But one thing we have learned is this: When children reach sixteen or seventeen years old, they make their own decisions. There is no more spanking or grounding or trying to get them to live as we want them to. They either choose to follow our guidelines and heed our advice, or they go their own way. We've often been heartbroken when children decided to do the latter, but we would not allow them to stay in our home while they were living in open rebellion against our rules. If they wanted to rebel, they had to go somewhere else to do it.

On occasion we sent children off to boarding schools or Christian living facilities to try to help them, but in most cases even that didn't work. For a time we had very little contact with some of these kids. They were bitter, struggling to get by, and blaming us for their plight. They thought we should be paying all their bills, buying their clothes, feeding them, and providing a car, but they didn't think it was fair of us to ask them to follow our rules in return. Life just doesn't work that way, so we let them find out the hard way. We think Dr. Campbell would probably agree that most antiauthority children have to find things out the hard way.

We continued to pray for our estranged children. We kept writing and calling them. We did our best to let them know that we loved them and cared about them, but we received few replies. Many nights we lay awake in bed wondering if they were okay. Were they eating right? Were they making it? How were they surviving?

When you have children like these, there seems to be a constant knot in your heart. But, oh, the joy when they return! We have some of these stories to relate as we go along. Thankfully, most of these difficult relationships have been restored, although we are still working on things in a few cases.

According to Dr. Campbell, pro-authority children are those whose basic approach to life is always, "What can I do to help?" Thank goodness we have eleven of these; eleven children who have followed our teaching—although, of course, not always perfectly. These children have listened and have begun to blaze their own trail in life. They made mistakes and tried our patience a time or two, but in the end they chose to experience things at the right times in life.

It is so satisfying to watch children like these and cheer them on. Stephen and Thomas, our twins from South Korea, graduated from the University of Florida in 2003 and are making their way through graduate school. Thomas is at Seton Hall University working on an MBA and a master's degree in sports administration. Stephen is going to the University of Massachusetts to obtain a master's in sports administration.

They have been a joy to raise and, as a result, have had some great experiences. During the summer after his sophomore year, Thomas studied abroad in Australia and Hong Kong through a university program. Another summer both boys had the opportunity to go back to South Korea and attend a university there for a few weeks. We encouraged them to stay for the entire summer and tour Asia. They had a wonderful time and learned a great deal about their origins. They loved it, and they told us they especially enjoyed being in a place where most people looked like them! (We sometimes forget that our children come from different cultures. We think of them simply as our children!)

As a college graduation present, we gave Stephen and Thomas a three-month tour of Europe. At twenty-two years old, they will have seen most of the world! We rejoice daily over their success and look forward to seeing what unfolds for them in the future.

The point we want to make here is that all of our children need to know that they are loved, cherished, respected, and honored in the same way. It is impossible for children to understand the depth and breadth of a parent's love. They can't comprehend how that love expands to include every child in the family. They seem to think that there's only so much love to go around and that it has to be divided by the number of children in the family. You may have to divide your time, but you don't have to divide your love. Now, we know quite well that every child is different. As parents, we always pray that the "good" differences will win out over the "bad" ones. But if you have a child, or a couple of children, who are driving you absolutely crazy, you're in pretty good company. Consider:

- **Albert Einstein** didn't speak a word until he was four years old.
- When **Thomas Edison** was six, he set his father's barn on fire.
- **Louis Pasteur** finished fifteenth out of twenty-two students in his chemistry class.
- **Pablo Picasso** had a very difficult time learning the letters of the alphabet.
- In his sophomore year at Harvard, **John F. Kennedy** received one B, four C's, and a D.
- **Ludwig Van Beethoven**'s piano teacher called him "a hopeless dunce."

We could go on and on with examples, but we're sure you get the point. Often the people who seem different or deficient in some way later make a contribution to the world.

The aggressive, adventuresome, disobedient child is harder to raise, that's for sure. But there's hope. Do you ever wonder what Bill Gates was like when he was a child? Don't you imagine his mother had her hands full? Imagine what it must have been like for Amelia Earhart's parents or for the nice couple in Italy, Mr. and Mrs. Columbus, who wanted their son Christopher to forget about all his silly dreams and go into the family business!

Now, of course, tolerating differences in children has its limits. We don't mean for a moment that we put up with laziness or foolishness. We've tolerated differences within certain parameters that everyone in the Williams family is expected to follow. We wouldn't, for instance, dream of letting one of our children demonstrate a unique perspective on life by cutting classes or refusing to do homework.

We've also made it very clear to every one of our kids that by the time they graduate from high school, they have to have a plan in place. They can go to college or a trade school, enlist in the service, or get a job, but they can't sit around trying to "find" themselves. Of course, we're willing to help as much as necessary, but we're not going to support our kids forever.

We agree with our friend Pastor Tony Evans, who sees a parallel between the parent-child relationship and our relationship with God:

> Parents can safely commit time, money, and other things to some children because they know they are going to do something good with what they've been given. With other children, the more money they are given, the more they waste it. The same is true for their time, educational opportunities, or any number of other benefits. It has nothing to do with the children's position in the family but with their practice as family members. God won't commit himself to some of us in terms of our discipleship because he knows we are going to wind up abusing his good gifts.

All children have gifts. Some simply don't use them or even search for them. What a waste! But that's the mystery of God's gift of freedom. Some will always choose the easy road; some will reach for the impossible.

Whichever category our children fall into, we constantly stress this principle with them: "You've got to approach life with confidence." This may mean that they do things they fear or aren't good at. But doing those things anyway builds character and confidence. Whether they are kids or adults, people naturally tend to think, "I can't do this, so I won't even try." Keep trying to drill confidence into your kids even when it doesn't seem to register. Then one day one of them will show you he got it!

My (Pat) son Bobby went into the baseball program at Rollins College as a freshman. He felt nervous and unsure of himself, not knowing whether he could play at that level. One day I went over to watch a scrimmage. Bobby was catching a wild left-handed pitcher. The young man on the mound was throwing curve ball after curve ball, all of them landing in the dirt. Afterward I took Bobby out to eat and said to him, "You must have had a tough time out there, catching for that kid who kept throwing curve balls in the dirt."

"Oh no," said Bobby. "I kept calling for more curve balls. I was hoping he'd throw 'em in the dirt and I'd get to show off my blocking ability to the coaches."

I grinned and said, "Bob, I love it!" It was exciting to see how much confidence he had gained and how he loved taking on a challenge.

You can't make children do what they don't want to do, and your children won't always meet your expectations, but when you extend them patience, love, and some coaching and cheerleading, you can open your children's minds to the wide-open, blue-sky possibilities that lie before them. And if all else fails, assure your kids you love them no matter what path they choose.

GO ONE ON ONE

Perhaps the very best way to ensure that your children know you love them (and to defuse discipline matters) is to spend time with them. This is not a new concept, but the point certainly bears repeating.

Like many other couples in these hectic times, we have schedules that are packed full. We both work full-time at jobs that sometimes require far more than forty hours a week. We both travel extensively for meetings, seminars, speeches, and book promotions.

Despite our busyness, we make it a point to spend one-on-one time with our children on a regular basis. No matter how cohesive and close the family might be, some things just can't be handled in a group situation. Every child needs a lot of one-on-one attention. She needs to have your undivided attention, to see that you are taking some time to listen to what is on her heart, and to know that she is really special and precious in your eyes—even if she does have eighteen brothers and sisters!

Several years ago, for example, Caroline wanted a special night with her daddy. Every year the Magic have a gala charity ball to raise money for the Orlando Magic Youth Foundation. It's called the Black Tie and Tennis Shoe Ball. Pat asked Caroline to be his date for the evening, and she was ecstatic. She dressed in a beautiful white ball gown with long white gloves and got to eat dinner with all the Magic players. What a night it was for her! She was thrilled by the opportunity to spend some time alone with her dad on a very special occasion. She looked like a princess and said later that she felt like one too. The other two girls at home are looking forward to their turn. Gabi will go next year and Kati the year after that.

Another such event happened earlier this year when Pat surprised Alan with a trip to an Atlanta Braves spring training game. After church one Sunday, Pat said, "Alan, come with me." Alan shot a quizzical look in Ruth's direction, as if to ask, "Am I in trouble for some reason?" Ruth just smiled and said, "Go on with your father," and off they went to the ball game.

Pat even took Alan down onto the field, where he was able to meet all the players and get some autographs. Then he got to see a great baseball game and, even more importantly, spend some quality time with his dad.

Gabi loves to watch movies, and so do I (Ruth). One of the things she and I do together is watch Lifetime Movies. Now that may not seem like a special thing to some people, but to Gabi and me, it's the greatest. We make popcorn, crawl up in my bed, and talk about what we're watching. I did the same thing with Stephanie when she was younger. In fact, even now in her thirties, she still loves to do this with me. Movies can be a great teaching tool. Things that happen on screen can open up conversations about real-life situations and decisions that must be made. During times like these, you get a chance to give your point of view on things, and you also get to hear your child's point of view. Believe me, you learn as much as your children do during such moments.

We have many more stories like these—memories of times when a particular child got to enjoy some time in the spotlight and special treatment from Mom or Dad. Such times are very important. It is also extremely important to spread them out equally among all your children. If you don't know what your children would like to do with you, ask! It might be anything from a ball game to a gala ball to simply watching a movie together at home.

There's only one way to make sure you're giving your children the attention they need, and that's to put them very high on your list of priorities (that means right after God and your marriage). It doesn't matter if you have one child or twenty, there will always be other "important" matters vying for your attention.

So, as far as we're concerned, if you find yourself unable to spend time with your children, then it's time to reprioritize your life. If you have to rid yourself of some commitments or activities to make time for your kids, then do it. We've had to! We've acted on our belief that spending time with our children is vitally important, no matter how old they are.

On June 10, 2003, our son Bobby celebrated his twenty-sixth birthday. Bobby is employed by the Cincinnati Reds and was coaching for their minor league team in Sarasota, a short drive down the Gulf Coast from the Tampa Bay area.

On Bobby's birthday Pat had a television interview scheduled in Tampa. In a fortunate "coincidence," the Reds were in St. Petersburg playing the Tampa Bay Devil Rays. Pat called Bobby and suggested that they go to the game together, which they did, and they had a terrific time. They were able to go down onto the field before the game to talk to some of the Reds' coaches and players, and Pat was even invited to throw out the ceremonial first pitch. A few days later, he got this note from Bobby: "Dad, thank you for sharing part of my birthday with me. I had a great time and loved being at a baseball game with you on my birthday. Love, Bobby."

As we said, your kids are never going to be too old to need and enjoy your attention. Remember that very few people have ever looked back over life from the vantage point of old age and wished they'd spent less time with their children.

Writing in *Christian Parenting Today,* Dr. John Trent says: "The more connected you are to your kids, the closer they feel to you. And the closer they feel, the more they'll open up their hearts to talk to you about their concerns, dreams, and prayers."

My (Ruth) office is at home. I can't tell you the number of times I've dropped whatever I'm working on to listen to a problem, answer a question, or share excitement over some special occurrence. Those times are priceless. I'll never forget the time my oldest daughter, Stephanie, came home from elementary school one day and asked me what a "bastard" was. She had heard another child use the word at school. Many people would be shocked and try to wash over it because it's not a nice word. But I believe you should face those things head on. If your children can't ask you about simple things, they won't bother with the big things. So I explained what the word meant.

As Stephanie grew older, she felt very comfortable talking with me about anything. In fact, all her friends came to me when they needed to talk.

Open communication with your children can start with something as small as defining a little, not-so-nice word and end up with a life-changing discussion about a career choice. Recently, for no special occasion, I got a card from Stephanie. It was a beautiful card, describing what a good mother is. On the card was a handwritten note that said, "Mom, you are my most favorite and cherished person in the world. I couldn't imagine having a better mom or friend. Thank you isn't enough for all that you do. I hope one day I am as great a mom and friend as you are to me. I love you. Stephanie."

You see, as parents, we simply have to be there for our children no matter how small or how large a decision they're facing. It's all about building the relationship, and that takes time and effort. But the payoff is enormous.

Writer Ray Pelletier said:

Kids need a "safety zone" in a confused and complicated world. They need a place of mental comfort and security. A haven where they know they're accepted and approved. They need a place where they can stop to get their bearings and sort out the influences that are seeking to control them—peer pressure, movies, TV—the whole world of twisted values in which money, sexual gratification, violence, craftiness, and self-serving often assume the proportions of saintliness.

From our point of view, we want the safety zone to be here at the Williams house. We want to be the sounding board, the place our children come to for sanctuary and advice, the place they truly call home.

PART THREE

Making Decisions
That Bless Your Children

Chapter 4

CHOICES PARENTS MAKE

I shall be telling this with a sigh,
Somewhere ages and ages hence;
Two roads converged in a wood and I—
I took the one less traveled by,
And that has made all the difference.
ROBERT FROST

Every parent makes dozens of choices every day, beginning with what time we get out of bed. Like many choices in life, this one is dictated by circumstances like what time we have to get the kids off to school, what time we have to get to the office, whether it's Monday morning or Saturday morning, and so on—but we still have some control over our decision.

Everyday choices like this one don't usually have any long-term ramifications. But some choices have far greater consequences. Why? Because our children are watching us. As author James Baldwin said, "Children have never been very good at listening to their elders, but they have never failed to imitate them."

Last year our daughter Gabi returned home after being away for several years getting special help. At first she had a difficult time adjusting to the new environment. Some of her brothers and sisters had left home during her absence, and the younger ones had grown up. Plus, at the age of seventeen, she wanted a lot of freedom that we were not willing to give her until she proved herself.

One evening I (Ruth) heard Gabi's voice coming from the room of her sister Caroline, who is one year older. Because I heard my name mentioned, I stopped outside the door and listened. What I heard warmed my heart and let me know that I had gotten through to Caroline. She was explaining the family rules to her younger sister, and it was almost as if I were listening to a tape recording of myself.

"Gabi, all you have to do is tell the truth," she said. "You'll get more privileges if you tell the truth. You'll only hurt yourself if you lie." She went on, listing all the reasons why Gabi ought to quit fighting us and start doing what we expected of her. She ended with, "Gabi, Mom loves you and wants to trust you. You just have to prove yourself. Listen to her. Do what she says. You'll be much happier."

Tears of joy welled up in my eyes and began to spill down my cheeks. Our children do imitate us—whether for good or bad. Whether we realize it or not, as parents we're almost always playing a game of follow-the-leader. Every move we make is on center stage, and our children are watching to see what we do.

What were the results of Gabi's conversation with Caroline? About six months after Gabi returned home, she wrote me the following letter:

Dear Mom,

I want to apologize for being very obnoxious to you. I feel bad for talking bad about you and also using you. I know that I should treat you with more courtesy. I'm sorry for taking all my anger out on you. Mom, I appreciate you helping me with my problems and talking to me about them. I realize that I've been treating you very badly, and from the heart, I'm sorry. I hope this letter means something to you and that you will accept my apology.

I love you very much,

Gabi

The victories, when they come, are oh, so sweet!

Robert E. Lee, too, gives us an example of how our children watch us. Lee was always regarded as a man of honor and integrity, even by those who fought against him during the Civil War. Late in his life he recalled an occasion that strengthened his resolve to be the best man he could possibly be.

The general was walking through snow, followed by his eight-year-old son, Custis. When Lee looked back to check on Custis, he was surprised to see how carefully the boy was following him. Custis was taking giant steps so that he could place his own feet in his father's footprints. Lee saw this as a metaphor for the parent-child relationship.

He said later, "When I saw this, I said to myself, *It behooves me to walk very straight when this fellow is already following my tracks.*"

Like Custis Lee before them, our children are constantly watching us, following the path we have marked out. Just as we were finishing this book, Bob Keeshan, Captain Kangaroo, died at age seventy-eight. Keeshan once said, "Parents are the ultimate role models for children. Every word, movement, and action has an effect. No other person or outside force has a greater influence on a child than the parent." For that reason, it is extremely important to maintain the following character traits in your life.

TELL THE TRUTH IN EVERY SITUATION

As we write this chapter, Martha Stewart is preparing to go to trial on charges that she was involved in insider trading with her friend Samuel Waksal, former chief executive of ImClone Systems. Waksal has already been sent to prison for defrauding his company's investors of millions of dollars.

James B. Comex, U.S. Attorney for the Southern District of New York, said: "This is a tragedy for the company and its six hundred employees. It's a tragedy that could have been prevented if those two people had only done what parents have taught their children for eons—that if you are in a tight spot, lying is not the way out. Lying is an act with profound consequences."

Young children tend to believe that anything their parents do is all right. Thus, if they hear us telling a lie, they'll get the idea that it's okay for them to lie too. An acquaintance tells us about the time she caught her eight-year-old daughter telling a fib to one of her playmates. Later on the woman took the little girl aside to explain that what she'd done was wrong.

"But Mom," she protested, "you lied to that man on the phone last night."

Mom was perplexed. "I lied? When did I do that, honey?"

"When you said Daddy wasn't home."

"But that was a telemarketer," her mom explained. "That was differ—"

Before she even finished the sentence, the mother realized that no situation justified lying.

"I'm sorry, honey," she said. "From now on I'm going to do my best not to lie anymore, and I want you to promise me you'll do the same thing."

"Okay, Mom," the little girl replied.

Smart mom.

SHOW INTEGRITY EVEN WHEN IT DOESN'T SEEM LIKE A SMART THING TO DO

Sports Illustrated recently ran a story about a seven-year-old boy named Tanner who plays Little League baseball in Wellington, Florida. It seems that Tanner, a first baseman, fielded a ball and tried to tag a runner going from first to second. When the umpire, a woman named Laura, called the runner out, Tanner ran up to her and told her that she was wrong. He had missed the tag. The ump reversed her call and sent the runner to second base. Tanner's coach, obviously a wise man, praised Tanner for being honest and gave him the game ball.

A couple of weeks later, Tanner was playing shortstop when a similar play occurred. This time Laura called a runner safe at third base, ruling that Tanner had missed the tag. The boy didn't protest. He just threw the ball back to his team's pitcher. But the look on his face showed his disappointment.

Laura called a time-out and asked him, "Did you tag the runner?"

Tanner nodded.

Again she reversed her call, this time from "safe" to "out." The coaches of the opposing team protested until she explained what had happened two weeks earlier. "If a kid is that honest, I have to give it to him," she said. "This game is supposed to be for kids."

Wouldn't it be great if that type of integrity were always rewarded, if we could raise up a new generation that valued truthfulness and honesty at all times?

Imagine that it's one of those Saturdays when you have a hundred things to do, and every item on your list is taking you twice as long as you thought it would. You and your two children—six and two years old—have just spent thirty minutes waiting in line at Target, and you have five more stops before you can finally head back home.

As you deposit your bags into the trunk of your car, a ninety-nine-cent package of candy tumbles out. You know you didn't pay for it.

"Where did this come from?" you ask.

Your six-year-old points at the two-year-old.

"She must have put it in your bag."

"Lisa! Did you put this in Mommy's bag?"

Lisa just stands there looking down at her shoes.

You know it will probably take you at least fifteen minutes to take the candy back into the store and explain to someone how it wound up in your bag. Besides, it's only a dollar. It's not like it will cause the entire Target chain to go out of business. Besides, the last time you returned some extra change to a cashier, she acted as if you were being a pain in the neck.

What will you do?

For your children's sake, you'd better take the candy back into the store. Why? Because it is in seemingly insignificant moments like this that our children are influenced by the choices we make.

One day, when Alan was at the grocery store with me (Ruth), I used my ATM card to pay the bill and told the cashier I wanted to get a hundred dollars back in cash. She handed me the money, which I slipped into my purse, and we walked out to the parking lot to put the groceries in the car. As we were preparing to drive away, I decided to put the money in my wallet. When I did, I discovered that the cashier had given me an extra twenty-dollar bill.

I sighed and said, "She gave me too much money. I'll have to go return it."

Alan shrugged. "Why don't you just keep it? It was their mistake."

"You're right," I said. "It was a mistake. But it would be a bigger mistake on my part to keep it. It wouldn't be honest. I'd be stealing."

Did it make a lasting impression on my son that I took the money back to the store? I don't know for certain. I hope so. But all we can do is plant the seeds and wait for them to grow. As Jesus said, even the smallest of seeds can grow into the biggest of plants (see Matthew 13:31-32).

Even though there may be times when it would be easier just to forget it and not worry about being a person of integrity, it is important for our children that we take the time to do the right thing in every situation.

When best-selling author Tom Peters spoke at a seminar in Orlando, he said, "There are no minor lapses in integrity." He was right. You either have it or you don't—and if you do, it will show up in everything you do. If you are a person of integrity, your children won't ever have any reason to question you. What's more, they just may copy your example, and the rest will be great history!

REFUSE TO GOSSIP OR TALK NEGATIVELY ABOUT PEOPLE BEHIND THEIR BACKS

Blaise Pascal may have been correct when he said, "I lay it down as a fact that if all men knew what others say of them, there would not be four friends in the world." But his statement cannot be used to justify joining in when talk turns to the shortcomings of others.

A friend named Nicole says she was shocked—and somewhat ashamed—when she heard her five-year-old daughter, Heather, talking on her toy telephone.

"She's such a phony," the little girl said. "Thinks she's smarter than anybody else," Heather continued in a cutting, sarcastic tone.

"Honey," Mom interrupted. "Who are you talking about?"

"Nobody," she answered. "I'm just playing."

Nicole remembers thinking, *Is that me? Am I the one who taught her to behave like that?*

She didn't want to be a critical, gossipy person, and she didn't want her daughter to be one either. She resolved right then that she would strive to change her behavior.

Like Nicole, we, too, have learned—again through experience—that we must be careful about what we say in front of our children. If we want them to have respect for others, then we have to show respect to others. That means we don't criticize the boss at the dinner table. We don't pick the teacher apart on the way home from school. We don't act one way to someone's face and another way behind his back. We strive to keep in mind what our mothers taught us: "If you can't say something good about someone, don't say anything at all."

If you, too, follow that advice, you'll be doing your children a huge favor.

SHOW COMPASSION TOWARD THE LESS FORTUNATE

In 2003 Jack Nicholson was nominated for the Best Actor Oscar for his role in the movie *About Schmidt*. He played a man who, reviewing his life from the vantage point of his retirement, felt that he had never accomplished anything of truly lasting value. Only when he sponsored a child through Childreach did he find the sense of purpose that always had eluded him.

Sponsoring a child is one of many ways you can teach your children about the importance of having compassion for others. We are partial to sponsorship because several of our children were born into extreme poverty in developing countries. We think of David, one of our sons from the Philippines. He is smart, fun loving, full of life, energy, and love. Yet, without our help, all of that energy and love probably would have been lost to the world.

We're not trying to pat ourselves on the back. Our point is that children everywhere have the same innate potential and the same capacity to give and receive love. But they all need a safe place to grow and an opportunity to show what they can do.

When you demonstrate compassion for the less fortunate, you are teaching your children that all human beings are of equal value, regardless of the circumstances in which they may find themselves. Some children are born in America to families with plenty of money. Others are born in the desert of Ethiopia to families struggling to survive. Some people are blessed with good health. Others are blinded or crippled by disease. Some people are naturally beautiful, while others could never make themselves very attractive no matter how hard they might work at it.

But the truth is that we are all made from dust, and we are all equally valuable in God's eyes. Active compassion—which means doing more than just feeling sorry for people—shows our kids that we understand the equal value of people and that we take to heart the Bible's command, "Carry each other's burdens, and in this way you will fulfill the law of Christ" (Galatians 6:2).

Work Hard to Attain Your Goals

Jonah, the grandson of one of Pat's college classmates, has a tool belt and a workbench out in the garage. Not bad for a guy who just celebrated his second birthday. One of his favorite tools is his handy-dandy power drill.

But before you start wondering who would be crazy enough to give a toddler an electric drill, we'd better explain that it doesn't have a real bit in it, just an ordinary wooden dowel. Even though his drill doesn't make holes in things, Jonah loves using it and his other tools because that's what his daddy does. Saturday afternoons will often find them working side by side in the garage, Dad at his workbench and Jonah at his, both of them intent on their latest projects.

Of course it's fun to see. But more significant, it's a reminder that children learn about the importance of hard work from their parents. Like Jonah's father, we have always tried to show our children that hard work can be fun, fulfilling, and the means to achieving important goals in life.

Gabi recently got hired by the beauty salon where her sister Caroline worked. Her job came as the result of a conversation Ruth had with the salon owner, Doug Adams. Gabi had turned in job applications at Kmart, an ice cream shop, and some grocery stores, but no one was hiring. When Ruth mentioned this to Doug, he said he needed some help a few hours a week.

When Ruth relayed this information, Gabi was so excited that she started jumping up and down. She began working two afternoons a week, and after only a couple of weeks, Doug was so pleased with her attitude and performance that he added an extra day to her schedule.

Recently, when Ruth was working in her office at home, the salon called and asked Gabi to come in immediately. They were suddenly swamped and needed extra help. Gabi's response was less than enthusiastic.

"Do I have to go?" she asked. "I don't feel like working today."

"Gabi," Ruth said, "it doesn't work that way. When you accept a job, you have to be ready when they need you. They gave you a chance when nobody else would, so when they call, you need to be excited about going in to work."

Ruth went on to tell her, "Gabi, understand that you will be working for someone for the rest of your life. You graduate from high school next year, and then it's go get some training and get to work. That's why Dad and I are always saying, 'Find something you love to do so you won't feel like you're working.' Instead you'll be having fun every day. That's how Dad and I feel about our jobs. We love working."

And we truly do! We agree with Thomas Edison: "I never worked a day in my life. It was all fun." That's how a career should be, and that's why we've tried so hard to direct our children into fields they love. Life is much more joyful and rewarding when you love what you do. As Voltaire wrote, "Work keeps at bay three great evils: boredom, vice and need."

STAY AWAY FROM HARMFUL ACTIVITIES SUCH AS DRINKING TO EXCESS OR SMOKING CIGARETTES

As writer Arnold Label says, "A child's conduct will reflect the ways of his parents." In other words, it doesn't do much good to say, "Do as I say, not as I do." Our conduct has more impact on our children than we can imagine. So,

- If you don't want your children to smoke, don't smoke yourself.
- If you don't want your children to drink, then don't do it yourself.
- If you don't want your children to smoke pot or experiment with other drugs, then don't use them yourself.

The Bible tells us that before we teach others—and this truth applies to our children—we need to have our own lives in order. Romans 2:21-22 says, "You who preach against stealing, do you steal? You who say that people should not commit adultery, do you commit adultery? You who abhor idols, do you rob temples?"

The apostle Paul also sent some advice to his young friend Timothy that all parents would do well to heed, urging him to "set an example...in speech, in life, in love, in faith and in purity" (1 Timothy 4:12).

Choose to Put Your Family First

Now that we have given advice about a number of specific choices parents can make, let's get to the real heart of the matter:

The best choice any parent can make
is to simply be there for his or her children.

It doesn't matter how busy you are or what you do for a living—whether you run a multinational corporation or put in eight hours a day on an assembly line in a factory. Nothing you do can possibly be more important than spending time with your children.

Writer Paul Lewis puts it this way: "When I ask older dads what their greatest regret is...and I ask this often...I have never heard: 'I regret I did not pursue my career more intensely,' but lots of men say, in one way or another, 'I regret that I did not take more time for my children when they were young and available to me and craved interaction. What I traded for those moments was not worth it.'"

Lee Iacocca was recognized as one of America's top corporate executives of the twentieth century. Among other accomplishments, he was credited with rebuilding the Chrysler Corporation, bringing it back from the edge of bankruptcy. Yet he says he always considered fatherhood his most important job. "I've seen a lot of executives who neglect their families, and it always makes me sad," he writes. "Hard work is essential. But there's also a time for rest and relaxation, for going to see your kid in the school play or at a swim meet."

He adds that, "If you don't do these things while the kids are young, there's no way to make it up later on." He concludes, "I've had a wonderful and successful career, but next to my family, it hasn't really mattered at all."

Evangelist Billy Graham first gained international fame over fifty years ago during a spectacular series of meetings in Los Angeles. Thousands of people, including many movie stars and other celebrities, came to hear Dr. Graham night after night for weeks. As the series entered its eighth week, Graham's sister-in-law and her husband came to Los Angeles, bringing a baby with them. The evangelist commented that the little girl was cute and asked to whom she belonged.

His sister-in-law's mouth dropped open in surprise. "Why...you," she replied.

Billy Graham had been away from home so long that he did not even recognize his own daughter, Anne. That night the great evangelist resolved that he would spend more time with his children.

As authors Henry and Richard Blackaby say, "No one could fault Graham for his work ethic or his godliness, but every [parent] could learn from his disquieting experience." Please don't make the mistake of thinking that you'll spend more time with your children "someday," because now is the only time any of us has.

Mike Martz, head coach of the St. Louis Rams of the National Football League, looks back over his children's growing-up years and regrets all the hours he spent away from home. "I was so goal-oriented," he says. "Gotta do this, gotta go, gotta go, gotta go. When I turned around and looked back, the years had flown by so quickly. The kids were grown, and I said to myself, 'Whoa. Let's put the brakes on and enjoy this thing as we go.' "

He adds, "That's what happens in coaching.... You can miss half of your kids' childhood. You have to include them in your life, and it's hard to do when you spend so much time at work."

Someone who has always had his priorities straight—family before career—is Karl Malone, a perennial all-star for the Utah Jazz and Los Angeles Lakers of the National Basketball Association. Despite all the attention and adulation he gets for his skills on the basketball court, Malone says he is happiest when he's just sitting around at home watching his children play.

He's not a big star to his kids. He's "just Dad," and that, Malone says, "keeps things in perspective for me." He adds that when his children are grown up, he doubts if they will remember watching him play basketball. "What they remember is when I go walking with them; when I go swimming with them; when I tuck them in at night. That's life...what it's about for me."

Another great athlete, Philadelphia Eagles all-pro cornerback Troy Vincent, has his priorities straight. Recently he said, "I don't let football define who I am. I'm a man, I'm a husband, I'm a father. I'm not afraid to wash dishes, take out the garbage, pump my own fuel, make my own bed."

Here are some more words of wisdom about the choices we parents have to make:

- **Laurel Cutler,** vice president of advertising agency Foote Cone & Bleding: "I wish I had known sooner that if you miss a child's play or performance or sporting event, you will have forgotten a year later the work emergency that caused you to miss it, but the child won't have forgotten that you weren't there."

- **Ben Stein,** actor, attorney, and aide to President Richard Nixon: "No corporate title can replace the times when your son leaned his head on your chest and fell asleep. No limousine or private jet makes up for being there when your son is growing from a child into a young man. Time spent with your child isn't a distraction from the main event. It is the main event."

- **Thomas Jefferson:** "The happiest moments of my life have been the few which I have passed at home in the bosom of my family."

- **Gabriella Marcella,** Argentine writer: "Many things in life can wait. But the child cannot. Now is the time when his bones are being formed, his blood is being made, and his mind is being shaped. His name is not tomorrow. It is today."
- **Theodore Roosevelt:** "For unflagging interest and enjoyment, a household of children, if things go reasonably well, certainly makes all other forms of success and achievement lose their importance by comparison."

I (Ruth) don't know who said this originally, but the bottom line of this chapter is simply this: "Keep the main thing the main thing." And the main thing for us parents is to be there to teach our children about life.

Chapter 5

STAND UP FOR YOUR FAITH!
THE MOST IMPORTANT
DECISION OF ALL

We must never be content with simply protecting our kids from the world. Rather, our goal should be to equip them to help change the world so that, when they go out into it, they do so as lights in the midst of darkness.

DR. TONY EVANS

A farming community in the Midwest was suffering through a time of terrible drought. Crops were withering in the fields. Disaster seemed imminent.

As fear grew, town leaders called everyone to gather in the town square to pray for rain. When the appointed day arrived, hundreds of people came to seek God's mercy. The day was cloudy, but that didn't mean much. There had been plenty of cloudy days lately, but that only made the dry weather seem worse. The clouds gave hope for relief, but they never delivered on their promise.

But on this day, after about an hour of urgent prayer, the sky began to darken. An excited cheer went up as a few drops of water fell from the sky. That's when everyone noticed the little boy, standing next to his mother, clutching an umbrella in his hand.

Suddenly the sky opened up, sending the drenched crowd scrambling for the shelter of their cars. Nobody had expected such an immediate and dramatic answer to their prayers—except that little boy! He knew it was going to rain, and it did.

That story reminds us about Jesus' teaching that anyone who wants to enter the kingdom of God must be like a little child and have a simple, trusting faith. (See Matthew 18:3-4.) It's our job, as parents, to help our children develop that kind of faith. If we do, their faith in God will sustain and support them all their lives. In order to foster such faith, we must live it out in front of our children. We believe that Christian parents should have the following goals to:

- lead each of our children to salvation through faith in Christ
- teach our children, by example, the importance of commitment to God and the church
- give our children an appreciation of the Bible as a guide for life
- teach our children the importance of obedience to spiritual authority

We love this quote from *Real Family Life* magazine: "Parents today need God's perspective of children. Children are divinely placed gifts, not accidents. They are a privilege. They are part of the life that God is bringing to us, every day. They are on loan with a divine purpose." The magazine goes on to say, "In the process of raising kids, it is easy to feel like you are just laying bricks. In reality, you are building a cathedral...a child whom God has given you to train up to carry on in the next generation. There is nothing more important in life."

FAITH MATTERS

Many people wonder, does faith make a difference in children's lives?

Absolutely. And we have proof.

Newspaper columnist Terry Pluto reports on a University of North Carolina study that looked at the lives of 2,478 kids between the ages of thirteen and seventeen. The overall conclusion was that kids who believe in God and attend church are much more likely to stay out of trouble. The study found that a youth's tendency to get into trouble was inversely related to the time he spent in faith-related activities. In other words, the more church services he attended, the more youth groups he was involved with, the more religious study he did, the less likely he was to get into trouble at school or with the law.

Pluto writes, "The report reveals that 'Religious 12th-graders' are less likely to drink and more likely to postpone their first time getting drunk. When they do drink, they are less likely to get drunk as compared to nonreligious 12th-graders." The study also found that teenagers who profess faith in God are "less likely to use drugs, less likely to engage in crime and violence, more likely to be involved in sports, student government, and other after-school activities. They usually have better relationships with their parents and are more likely to volunteer for community projects."

Pluto goes on to say, "Even 'good kids'—from homes where all the basic needs are met and there is plenty of extra cash and goodies to go around—are looking for something they can believe in, something more than getting a good job, a nice house, and a healthy paycheck.

"Why?

"It's not about stuff. It's about faith. It's about believing in a God who tells us how to live.

"Some people will use the National Study of Youth & Religion as a vehicle to promote school prayer, but the real question isn't whether we pray in school. It's whether we pray at home. The home is the first church. The home is the first place kids get their image of God. The home is where faith and values must be taught."

Amen!

Now, we're not saying that bringing up your kids in an atmosphere of faith is a surefire way to keep them out of trouble. We know some kids who have grown up in God-fearing, churchgoing families, but they have made complete messes out of their lives anyway. We can't offer ironclad guarantees. But it's generally true that kids who are raised in families where faith is important turn out better than those raised in families where faith isn't important.

Our friend Bobby Malkmus has always been an inspiration to us in matters of faith. Looking back on fifty years of marriage to his wonderful wife, Ruth, Bobby says, "We've had our disappointments, struggles, setbacks, but with each one we've been made stronger and our faith has increased. Our children have benefited from a Christ-centered home. Even today our [adult] children thank us for that upbringing. To God be the glory!"

How can we build faith in our children? Here are several ways:

- Show them a godly example.
- Let them see God in you.
- Tell them what you believe and why you believe it.
- Pray for them and with them.
- Study the Bible with them.
- Make church a habit.
- Stand up for the truth and help them do the same.

Show Them a Godly Example

Pastor/author David Mains says he has come to the conclusion that "the best way I can improve my children's spiritual lives is to continually improve my own."

That's a great thought, and it goes hand in hand with this one from Larry Christenson: "Happy is the child who happens in upon his parent, from time to time, to see him on his knees…or going aside, regularly, to keep times with the Lord."

It's vital for our children's spiritual health that they see in us the characteristics of Christian behavior, such as righteousness, unselfishness, and truthfulness. Remember that what your children see you do is of more significance than what they hear you say. That's why it's very important for parents to spend time with God in Bible study and prayer, asking him to develop his character within us. Howard Hendricks says that if your Christianity doesn't work at home, it doesn't work, and he is absolutely correct.

We must strive to show our children that our faith in God is important to us. It's not just a Sunday thing. It's how we live. We want them to know that our faith is what sustains us during difficult times, gives us hope when the future looks scary, and lifts us up when the world tries to drag us down. In good times, faith is what keeps us where we need to be and validates our decisions. The best definition of faith we've ever heard comes from the gifted pen of author Philip Yancey. He wrote, "Faith means believing in advance what will only make sense in reverse."

One of the ways we live out our faith is through tithing. This means we give 10 percent of our income to God, as he asks us to do in the Bible (see Malachi 3:8-12). The children watched us put our envelope in the plate every Sunday for years. Then they began to earn their own money. Caroline got a job at a beauty salon as an assistant. Kati weeds the flower beds each week. Alan gets paid as a ball boy for the Orlando Magic. Gabi helps out with the housework and also works in a salon.

One of the things we have insisted on from the very beginning is that they give 10 percent of their income to the church. At first they weren't very happy about that.

"Ten percent! That's way too much!" was a very typical reaction.

But we explained that this was God's rule and added that he also asks us to give cheerfully (see 2 Corinthians 9:7). The looks on their faces weren't all that cheerful, but we insisted, so what else could they do? They gave a bit grudgingly at first. But they gave. Over time they began to experience the joy that naturally comes from giving. On the way to church Sunday morning, one of them always says, "Mom, I've got my envelope!" I (Ruth) always answer, "Me too!"

It is our hope that the principle of tithing will become ingrained in our children and that they will continue to live out their faith in this way when they are grown and on their own. We know from many personal experiences that when you follow God's guidelines, he always provides. Let us explain. Since we both depend on speaking engagements for much of our income, we never know what our financial situation is going to be. There are times when our calendars are completely full. But there are also some slow times when our income might not be quite enough to meet the expenses of our average-sized, nineteen-children family. But we have always given our tithe and depended upon God to get us through. And he has always come through.

Several years ago, for instance, our church had a building program to expand the services we could offer to the community. One particular piece of property was extremely hard to purchase, and it stood in the way of expansion. The church prayed earnestly that God would make a way for us to buy this piece of land.

The two of us spent quite a bit of time discussing what we should give in addition to our tithe. We really wanted to participate because we knew that many lives would be affected by this new ministry, but our income had been lower than usual for the past few months.

One Sunday we prayed about the situation and promised God that if he would give Pat some speaking engagements, we would give the first $10,000 to the building program. Almost immediately calls started coming in from people who wanted to book Pat for a speech. We were so excited when we wrote the check for $10,000 and placed it in the offering plate. It was wonderful to see God working and to be able to give back a portion of what he had given to us.

Let Them See God in You

There are two very important reasons why your children should see your determination to live a godly life. First, it shows them that your faith is truly important to you. Your modeling will make faith more important to them too. Second, as Dr. James Dobson says, "A child identifies his parents with God, whether the adults want that role or not. Most children 'see' God the way they perceive their earthly fathers."

Steve Farrar, writing in *New Man* magazine, quotes Proverbs 20:7: "A righteous man who walks in his integrity—How blessed are his sons after him" (NASB). Farrar goes on to say, "God gives every father [and mother] the opportunity to do something great. It is the wise [parent] who makes the most of this opportunity. I'm convinced that God doesn't expect us to just take care of our families today, but He wants our leadership to be so noble that it will carry our families for at least a solid century."

Showing your kids a godly example also involves showing them something of God's unconditional love. In their book *How to Be a Christ-Shaped Family,* Myron and Esther Augsburger write, "Love gives to family members a sense of belonging…the security of worth, and the enrichment of spirit. The security of love is expressed by God himself in Isaiah 49:16: 'I have engraved you on the palms of my hands.' What a beautiful image of the Sculptor's love. To love and be loved expresses the greater privilege of humanness…of being persons who share the image of the Divine."

Strive to show your children, through your actions, how very much God loves them.

Tell Them What You Believe and Why You Believe It

Although we just pointed out that what you do is more important than what you say, what you *say* is still important. Some parents make the mistake of thinking that their children just naturally understand why they are Christians. But how can our children know unless we tell them?

Do your children know what you believe? Do they know why you made a decision to follow Christ? Do you have a testimony about how you began living a life of faith? If so, your children need to hear it.

Following his appearance in the 1997 World Series, Minnesota Twins pitcher Mike Jackson said, "It meant so much to fulfill a childhood dream, but those feelings are temporary. The World Series was great to be a part of, but it was only seven games that took seven days of my life. My relationship with Christ is much more meaningful because it will last an eternity."

Has God brought joy and meaning into your life? If so, please tell your children how you feel! You can't make your children believe in God. You can't believe for them. That is something they have to do on their own. But you can certainly make it easier for them to believe. You can point them in the right direction and give them opportunities to hear his Word.

You can trust him to do the rest. He will.

Pray for Them and with Them

We make it a habit to pray for our children every day—and not just in our private devotion time. When one of our children is worried about something, we'll ask, "Would you like us to pray about that?" Sometimes we don't even ask the question. We just say, "Let's take a moment to pray about that."

That was the case when Pat drove Gabi to take her driver's drug and alcohol test. In Florida teenagers must pass this rather lengthy test before they can get their first driver's license. Pat noticed that Gabi was nervous, so before he dropped her off, he told her that he wanted to pray with her. After doing so, he walked her to the classroom where she was to take the test. Four hours later, when Pat returned to get her, Gabi literally danced out of the classroom with the happy news that she'd passed the test.

As she climbed into the car, she said, "Dad, about that prayer. That stuff works, doesn't it?"

Yes, Gabi, it does!

Praying with our kids and for them is a key way we live in faith. When we pray with our children and share from our hearts, we show them that our faith is real. They can see that it is an everyday thing, not something that comes and goes. Whenever there's an important decision to be made, the first thing we do is pray about it. When someone is sick, we pray. When we're facing a problem of any kind, we pray, and then we trust God to handle it as he sees fit.

Our kids also know that we pray when things are going well, thanking God for the gifts he's given us. We know that we depend on God for everything, and we want our children to know it too. That is one reason why we so appreciate this quote from the late Gen. Douglas MacArthur:

> By profession, I am a soldier, and take pride in that fact, but I am prouder—infinitely prouder—to be a father. A soldier destroys in order to build. A father only builds; never destroys. The one has the potentiality of death; the other embodies creation and life. While the hordes of death are mighty, the battalions of life are mightier still. It is my hope that my son, when I am gone, will remember me, not from the battle,

but in the home, repeating with him our simple daily prayer, "Our Father, Who art in heaven…"

Study the Bible with Them

Perhaps you have heard of Allyson Felix. If not, you probably will sooner or later. Allyson is a rising young track phenom who is currently recognized as the fastest woman in the world in the 200-meter sprint.

Allyson's father, Paul, says, "We're Christians, so we've used the Bible to teach values to our kids. I think they've taken what we've taught them to heart, and that's helped them keep things in perspective. Allyson's running is fleeting. At some point, it's going to be over."

Allyson's brother Wes, a track star in his own right, has this to say: "We've always had the understanding that it's just sports. All it takes is one injury or a car accident and it could be over, so don't take it too seriously. It's a great opportunity to do some things and travel to some interesting places, but it's still just sports."

Then, talking about his sister, he adds, "She's the same sweet person she has always been, and that's the thing I'm so proud of." There's that biblical foundation again.

Ron Corielli, of Cedarville College in Ohio, suggests several ways parents can use the Bible to help their children be the people God intended them to be. He says parents should:

- Read Scripture to our children, if only for a few minutes a day.
- Use Scripture to provide guidance, remembering that, as the Bible says, "Your word is a lamp to my feet and a light for my path" (Psalm 119:105).
- Comfort children with Scripture during times of trouble.
- Help your children memorize Scripture.
- Use the Bible to help your children see their need for a Savior.

Make Church a Habit

Ruth says: During the Christmas season a couple of years ago, my oldest daughter, Stephanie, went with me to New Orleans to visit my brother, Burke, his wife, Diane, and their three children. Burke and Diane are true role models as parents.

At lunch one day we got to talking about parenting, and my brother gave Stephanie some great advice. He said, "The most important thing you can do as a parent is take your children to Sunday school and church every Sunday."

Pat and I agree. Church attendance is mandatory in the Williams house. You can just imagine what it's like trying to get nineteen kids out of bed and ready for Sunday school. Sometimes it feels like one of those dreams where you're running as fast as you can and not getting anywhere. Yes, we occasionally feel like giving up and going back to bed. But we don't.

We attend church, first of all, because it honors God. We know the importance of acknowledging God's involvement in our lives and showing him the love and respect he deserves. Plus, he tells us to come together regularly to worship him, so we do. It's the very least we can do in response to all the blessings he's given us.

To be honest, however, not all of our children have always shared our enthusiasm for church attendance. At times one or another of them has been like the preacher's son who jumped out of bed one Saturday morning and proclaimed excitedly, "Oh boy! Today's not the day we have to go to church!" Be that as it may, we've always made it understood that anyone who lives under our roof must go by our rules, and one of those rules is regular church attendance. Our hope is that, by the time they are out on their own, they will continue to attend church, not for us, but for themselves and for God.

Dr. Jay Strack told us that research shows that 88 percent of our young people stop attending church when they go off to college. They choose to sleep in on Sunday mornings. It's not that they suddenly become anti-Christian. It's just that church doesn't excite them. They'd simply rather sleep. However, the good news is that many of them return to church when they have their own children.

We don't think you should bug your adult children about church. So what do we do? We drop hints from time to time. For example, Pat might ask a question like, "Stephen, how was church in Gainesville on Sunday?" It used to be that when Stephen heard that question, he'd respond with an embarrassed laugh. He wasn't going to church, and we knew it. In fact for several years, neither Stephen nor Thomas attended church unless they were spending some time at home with us.

But we didn't give up, and neither should you. The good news is that about a year ago Stephen didn't come home one weekend, and when we asked Thomas why, he told us, "He's at a church retreat." We were so happy. Now Stephen even plays guitar in a little church group.

Stand Up for the Truth and Help Them Do the Same

When Karyn was twenty-one, she was a junior at the University of Florida, majoring in broadcast journalism. Her goals at that juncture of her life were to either be a professional singer or the next Katie Couric. We were her biggest cheerleaders—and still are.

Now, this may sound like boasting, but it's simply the truth. Karyn has it all: beauty, talent, and a sweet disposition. So we weren't surprised when she entered and won the 2001 Miss University of Florida Beauty Pageant. Next stop after that was the Miss Florida contest and then, hopefully, the Miss America Pageant.

That same year she met her husband, Dale, and they fell instantly in love. The day after she met him, she called to tell us she had met the man she was going to marry. We told her to take it slowly, to get to know him—all the things you would expect concerned parents to say.

Over the next few weeks Karyn worked very hard to get ready for the Miss Florida pageant, and we got to know and love Dale too. It turned out that he was something of a fitness fanatic, and he devoted hours to helping Karyn get into the best possible physical condition. By the time the pageant arrived, there wasn't a single ounce of fat on her.

She also worked with a voice coach to put the finishing touches on the song she planned to sing. Our friend Jeanette Hughes, who had worked with the Miss Florida Pageant in the past, coached her on pageant etiquette and traditions.

Also, because Pat is an experienced interviewer, he helped Karyn get ready for that part of the competition. He asked her dozens of questions about current events, her personal life, and her plans for the future.

Everyone's hard work paid off beautifully. Throughout the week of the pageant, Karyn consistently won the interview competition. She also won the talent and evening gown competitions. We were so proud of her, not only because she was so beautiful and so poised, but because we knew how very hard she had worked to prepare for this big moment in her life.

On the evening of the final competition, we were sky-high with excitement and anticipation. Dozens of our friends and family members were in the audience, and we had all heard the rumor that Karyn was the one to beat. We were sitting right up front as the ten finalists were announced. As we expected, Karyn was among them.

Our pride grew as the evening went along. She sang perfectly. She looked stunning in her evening gown and swimsuit. We were all on the edge of our seats when the emcee announced that Karyn was one of the five finalists.

There was only one last hurdle to clear, and that was answering the final question that would help the judges determine the winner. Since she had already won the previous interview competition, we were confident that our daughter was about to be crowned Miss Florida! What an exciting moment that was!

We knew that the final question usually covered the contestant's platform. In Karyn's case, the subject was international adoption. She was certainly ready for that one! And because she was going to be the last finalist questioned, we expected that the evening would build to a stupendous finish.

The other finalists all gave good answers to their questions, which were fairly easy. One girl was asked, "Should high-school students be required to do community service?" Another was asked, "Should students be required to wear school uniforms?"

Finally it was Karyn's turn. This was it! We were waiting for her to give the winning answer and move on to the Miss America Pageant.

Then came a question no one expected: "Karyn, the Southern Baptist

Convention was in town last week, and they have decided that women should not be allowed to be pastors. How do you feel about that subject?"

A collective gasp arose from the audience, followed by a displeased murmur. Behind us someone whispered, "What kind of question was that?"

Karyn was obviously thrown off balance. Shock showed on her face. The question had nothing to do with her platform but instead referred to her personal religious convictions. We are Baptists, and Karyn was raised in that denomination. Perhaps the judges were expecting Karyn to speak out on behalf of women's rights. But for Karyn, the question went deeper than opinion.

After the auditorium quieted down, Karyn said firmly, "I don't feel that women should be pastors because the Bible is very clear about it. Men should be the leaders of the church."

Again the audience gasped in unison. We all knew that Karyn wasn't saying what the judges wanted to hear. We were gratified and pleased that she was standing up for what she believed in, but we were disappointed that she had been thrown such a curve ball. We just hoped that the rest of the week's competition would be enough to give her the edge.

Now it was time to announce the winner.

Fourth runner-up.

Karyn was still standing on stage!

Third runner-up.

She was among the final three!

Second runner-up.

It was down to Karyn and one other young woman!

"First runner-up is…Karyn Williams!"

You can't imagine the emotional high that comes from reaching that point. But neither can you imagine the letdown that comes from hearing your name announced as first runner-up.

We were so proud of our daughter at that moment, but we were also devastated that her personal beliefs may have cost her the opportunity to represent the state of Florida in Atlantic City. But we trust God's perfect plan for Karyn to be worked out, even with a disappointment like this. Karyn could have returned to the pageant the following year, but instead she got married. Since then she has acquired a real estate license and completed college. We are so proud of her.

We agree with Ruth Bell Graham when she said, "Children are facing temptations and pressures we never had to face—instead of 'Thou shalt not...' it is 'Why not...?' Teach your children the Word of God as soon as they can talk.... Young people are confused. We turn our children out in high-powered cars onto the highway of life without road rules, road signs, guardrails, centerlines, and with faulty brakes and wonder why there are so many wrecks.... Your children need love, appreciation, and guidance—love your children and let them know it."

Chapter 6

How to Help Your Children

Make Right Choices

All kids need is a little help, a little hope, and somebody who believes in them.

FORMER NBA STAR EARVIN "MAGIC" JOHNSON

There's a little phrase that every parent knows. Over the past few years, we must have heard it at least a hundred times. We're pretty sure kids have been saying it to their parents for at least a thousand years. And if the world lasts that long, they'll be saying it for at least a thousand more: "But everybody's doing it!"

Are you nodding your head in recognition? If you haven't heard those exact words coming out of your child's mouth, you've probably heard one of the many variations, such as:

- "Everybody's going to be there."
- "Everybody's wearing their hair this way."
- "Everybody's wearing their skirts this short."
- "Everybody gets to stay out later than I do."
- "Everybody gets a bigger allowance than I do."

Now, it may be true that "everybody's doing it," whatever it is, but over the years, we've discovered that this doesn't mean our kids have to do it too— or that we have to sanction it. But how do we parents get our children to choose the road less traveled in a world where peer pressure is king? That's the question up for discussion in this chapter.

One of the things I'm (Ruth) happiest about is that my oldest daughter, Stephanie (now in her thirties), has never smoked or tried drugs. A few years ago she was dating a young man. As they got to know each other, they both discovered that neither one of them had done any drugs while growing up. That is so unusual today with all the peer pressure and cultural encouragement to try drugs. I'm so proud of her for sticking to her convictions and always saying no. It's nice to know that some kids do say no in spite of the negative influences around them.

How powerful is peer pressure? Cathy Brundage, writing in the *Arizona Republic*, tells a story that makes the power of peer pressure chillingly clear:

> I was in a college psychology class when I learned about the real meaning of peer pressure. Our professor had the class demonstrate how peer pressure works. He asked ten students to leave the room. He instructed the remainder of us to create a consensus against what was clearly the truth. When our professor held up a red square, we were to agree that it was green.
>
> When the ten students returned to the classroom, our teacher held up the red square. "Raise your hand if you see a green square." We all raised our hands, including six of the ten students who had left the classroom. There was a general uneasiness in the room. All of the ten students looked uncomfortable, especially the ones who had raised their hands, pretending that they had seen a green square. "That," my professor gloated, "is peer pressure. The power of group dynamics can get the individual to do just about anything."

What a powerful lesson for those of us who want to help our kids steer the proper course through life even if no one else agrees with what we're doing.

Study after study shows that in families where there is good communication, the chance of children getting involved with drugs, alcohol, sex, or crime diminishes greatly, as does the suicide rate. This doesn't mean it never happens, but the chances are much less.

But what exactly do we mean by good communication? We mean a family in which everyone invests something of himself—a family where everyone comes together regularly to openly talk, listen, laugh, cry, and learn about what is going on in each other's lives. In our family good communication takes place as we pray together or have family discussions about current issues when we sit around the dinner table. The best times of all are the fun, relaxed times. These are the moments when family bonds are strengthened and lifelong memories built.

Now you may be thinking to yourself, *Peer pressure wasn't that big of a deal when I was a kid.* Really? Have you ever been flipping through an old photo album and come across a picture of yourself wearing something that made you look like a candidate for Geek of the Year? It's always startling at first. And then you remember that everybody was doing it! Sure it was stupid looking or uncomfortable. But then, as now, peer pressure often took precedence over common sense.

So when the time comes for your children to strike out on their own, what will help you know they're going to make intelligent, well-thought-out choices about things like money, sex, faith, friends, career, drugs and alcohol, tobacco, and diet? Let's take a brief, closer look at each of these areas.

MONEY

We believe that children should learn to handle money as soon as they're old enough to understand how it works. The spending habits they learn now will likely stay with them the rest of their lives. For example, when our children were younger, they were required to do certain chores to earn an allowance. Once the allowance was given, it had to last the entire week until the next payday; there were no cash advances or bailouts. During that week the child had to choose how much to spend, how much to save, and how much to give to God.

At first young children want to spend their money as soon as they get it. But when we let them suffer the consequences of reckless spending, they learn pretty quickly how to be good money managers.

Sometimes, as our children get older, they have to learn practical lessons about money. For example, Caroline recently got married. Her husband, Dimitry, is a brand-new-to-the-navy recruit. Ruth just hates to take on the role of spoilsport, but as we were planning the wedding, she couldn't help but ask: "Caroline, how much money are you and Dimitry going to need each month to make ends meet?"

Caroline's response: "I don't know."

"Caroline, how much money do you and Dimitry make?"

"Enough."

That was her answer: "Enough." But what does enough mean? She could not answer, but at least that opened up a discussion of how to do budgets and what it takes to run even a small, new household. Caroline has a lot to learn, and we've had fun working through it with her.

Just as important for children to learn how to budget their money is for them to learn how to use credit cards properly. We are constantly amazed at the number of "free" credit card applications our kids get in the mail, some of them directed to children under eighteen. We throw them away immediately.

But every once in a while, one of them slips through. Recently one of our children was practically jumping up and down with excitement. "Look! I got a credit card in the mail, and it's free!"

"Wow!" we said. "That is exciting, isn't it? Let's sit down and talk about what this means."

"It means I can buy stuff and don't have to pay, right?"

"Not exactly, sweetheart. It means you get a bill every month, and if you don't pay the whole amount, the credit card company charges you interest. Each month that interest keeps increasing until you owe double or triple the cost of the item you charged in the first place."

"Wow, I didn't know that. I guess I really don't want one after all." Whew!

We won that round, but we hate to think of all the children who fall for the "free" credit card and don't even get out of childhood before they're in debt. Then the spiraling continues, and they have bad credit and can't buy a car or a house when the time comes—all because they were enticed by a company preying on young people who don't yet know any better.

Clearly, one of the key financial lessons we must teach our children is how to stay out of debt in our consumer-oriented, have-it-now, pay-for-it-later society.

Sometimes we're successful in our efforts to get through to our kids, and sometimes children who have learned for themselves teach the others. We recently had a visit from Sarah who was just turning twenty-three. She wanted to talk to us about returning to school. She needed a little financial help, and we were discussing how we could best give it to her.

She said that she wanted to move closer to her job and school because her car was in bad shape and had left her stranded a few times. Because that car was completely paid off, we suggested that she pursue the possibility of trading it in for something newer and more reliable. Her response was that she would have a hard time getting approved for a car because her credit was so bad.

"Why is that?" we asked.

"I didn't pay some of my bills on time."

"Do you have any credit cards?"

"Oh no," she replied. "Andrea would never let me have one of those."

We laughed. You see, Andrea is Sarah's younger sister by one year. They were adopted from South Korea at ages two and three. Even though Sarah is older, Andrea has always been the more practical, levelheaded, and organized of the two. Since they've been out on their own, Sarah has always relied upon Andrea for advice.

When Sarah told us that her sister wouldn't allow her to have a credit card, we were both thinking, "Way to go, Andrea!" She had obviously learned the lesson well.

SEX

Today's kids are bombarded by sex from a very early age. It's on television. It's in music. It's in movies. There is just no way to shield them from it. But we want our children to know more about sex than just the mechanics of it. We want them to understand that sex is something sacred and beautiful, a gift from God. We also want them to know that sex is not a toy and that when misused, it can lead to emotional, physical, and spiritual destruction. (Just look at the devastation in sub-Saharan Africa: AIDS has killed off much of an entire generation of parents and left eleven million orphans in its wake.)

We doubt that it has ever been more difficult to maintain a pure sexual life than it is today. When we were kids, sexual purity was pretty much "in." Oh yes, there were the "bad boys" who were admired for their sexual prowess (much of it exaggerated, to be sure), but there was not much pressure on the rest of us, and especially not on girls, to lose their virginity. These days we understand that for the most part virgins are looked down on as geeks and nerds. Even though times have changed, God's instructions have not.

If we want our children to follow God's teaching, we must talk to them about life—even when it's difficult or awkward. Sex education at school isn't enough, and it doesn't cover what God says. Sunday school doesn't hit it very hard either. Our children have to hear the truth about sex from us. And we have to be open.

Ruth recalls: One weekend Kati, age seventeen, had her best friend, Michelle, over to spend the night. We were just hanging out in the kitchen when Michelle suddenly asked, "Do you and Mr. Williams still have sex?"

Without skipping a beat I answered, "Of course. Why would you ask that?"

"Well, you have enough kids," she said. "Why would you?"

I smiled and said, "Because, Michelle, I love him. He loves me. Sex is not just about having kids. It's one of the ways married couples show their love for each other."

She said, "Well, I'm really scared about having sex."

I said, "That's natural for a girl your age. That's because it's not the right time for you. You're too young and you're not married. Sex is one of the most wonderful things in the world—if you're married. It's a very special bond between two people."

"But do you have to be married?" she asked.

"Some people who have sex aren't married," I told her, "but God says we should be, and I think sex is much more beautiful when it's done God's way."

"Thanks for talking to me," she said.

We can't guarantee that our kids will remain sexually pure until marriage, as God intended. But we can and do teach them that this is God's way. This is a topic I (Ruth) discuss over and over again with our daughters. I just hope it registers.

And most parents feel that way. That's why Pat gets phone calls all the time from desperate parents looking for advice. Recently he got a call from a single mother of three children. She said she was having some problems with her middle child, a thirteen-year-old boy who had just finished the eighth grade.

Pat asked, "Is he messing up in school?"

"Oh no," the woman answered. "He's a terrific student." Before Pat could ask if he was being disrespectful or disobedient, she added, "He's a wonderful boy with a great personality."

"Well then, what's wrong?"

"Every night at seven o'clock, the phone rings, and it's a girl wanting to talk to him," she explained. "As soon as he gets off the phone, it rings again, and it's another girl. This goes on all evening long, one phone call after another."

Pat laughed, "Sounds like your son is a pretty popular guy."

The woman sighed and said she hadn't minded so much that the girls were calling until she leafed through her son's yearbook. Then she gasped when she saw what some of these twelve- and thirteen-year-old girls had written. One wrote, *Please don't go to bed with anyone else this summer. I want to be the first.* Another wrote, *I can't wait to —— you.* Several others wrote similar comments.

"How can I make my son understand that sex is reserved for marriage?" the woman asked. "I'm not sure if he can resist that kind of pressure and temptation."

In order to protect her son, this single mom took a couple of drastic measures. She blocked her phone from receiving calls from certain numbers. And she arranged with her ex-husband to have the boy spend his ninth-grade year with him so he'd have a strong male influence in his life. She hated the fact that her son wouldn't be with her, but she decided that was better than seeing him enter into destructive and sinful sexual relationships.

This mother's dilemma is just another indication of our society's preoccupation with sex. Our children are constantly bombarded with sexual images and messages. It's up to us to teach them that sex is something sacred, that it is not a toy, and that it is not intended for children.

FAITH

We've already mentioned that we talk to our kids about God, pray with them, and show them in other ways that our faith is important to us. In a world full of spiritual confusion, we are convinced it is very important for our children to understand what we believe and why we believe it.

We've heard some people say that they're going to let their children make up their own minds about religion, but that approach always strikes us as rather silly. You wouldn't let a young child eat anything he wanted because he probably wouldn't eat things that are good for him. You wouldn't let him decide what time to go to bed at night because he wouldn't get enough sleep. You wouldn't let him decide how often to take a bath or brush his teeth because he'd probably never do either! Indulging a child in any of those ways would be detrimental to his physical health.

So why would you take chances with a child's spiritual health, which is far more important? It's true that we can't believe in God for our children. Faith is a choice that everyone has to make for herself. But we want to do everything we can to make sure our children choose wisely.

Friends

Choosing the right friends are some of the most important choices your child will ever make. The Bible says, "Do not be misled: 'Bad company corrupts good character' " (1 Corinthians 15:33). And La Rouchefoucauld wrote, "A true friend is the greatest of all blessings."

Remember that kids tend to choose friends whose values and behavior support their own. So when a kid gets into trouble because of peer pressure, you can't simply blame the peers. The child has made choices that have placed him in that peer group, and the child is responsible for those choices. As parents *we* are responsible for knowing who our children's friends are and for helping them choose the right ones so that negative pressure won't even take place. We have to help our children put up guardrails that can keep them from going over the edge. One thing we can do is make sure our children have the best possible opportunity to choose friends from families who share our beliefs, convictions, and high moral standards. That's why we make sure they're involved in activities such as Scouting, church youth groups, organized sports, dance programs, academic clubs, and so on.

But we've discovered that the most important thing you can do is talk to your children about their friends. Whom do they hang out with? What do they like most about their friends? Do their friends ever try to get them to do things they know they shouldn't do? What do they dislike about their friends?

We always show interest in our children's friends—and, yes, we sometimes become detectives. For example, whenever one of our kids asks to go to a friend's house, we always ask for the home phone number and then put in a follow-up call to the parents. We want to make sure that the visit or activity is approved and that the parents will be home. There have been times when the parents we called had no idea there were any plans (imagine that!) or else were not going to be home.

In fact, one day I (Ruth) called and talked to the father of a friend of Gabi's. I told him I was just checking to make sure he'd be home for the slumber party. He was shocked because I was the *only* parent who had called.

Our rule is that we do not allow anyone to spend the night at someone else's house unless the parents are going to be there. Are we old-fashioned? You bet! But we explain to our kids that we don't want to put them in a situation that could be compromising. They simply don't need that pressure. We do a lot of checking up, but it's worth it. And believe it or not, it's almost always appreciated by the other parents—and even by our children. Our effort lets our kids know that we love them and are concerned about their welfare.

Also, whenever we see one of our children's friends behaving in a way that bothers us, we talk to our son or daughter about it. We let our child know that we're disappointed in that kind of behavior and explain why. We try hard not to be judgmental or overly critical, yet we know that while the best kind of friends can be a blessing, the wrong kind of friends can be a curse.

Because that is true, we have at times made a person off-limits. That course of action may seem extreme, but the consequences of not doing so would be the same as allowing a child to play in the middle of a busy street. In the final analysis, if your children cannot choose the right people as friends, you have to do what you can to ensure that they do not choose the wrong ones.

And over the last few years, we've had several such incidents. One involved Alan. He had been doing great in school, and his attitude had been terrific. Things were progressing very nicely.

Then a new boy came to Alan's school.

Alan really liked Chuck. He invited him over several times to spend the night, and he seemed like a nice boy. Then one weekend Alan went over to Chuck's house. Several weeks later, we got a phone call from Chuck's mother telling us that the boys had been caught making obscene phone calls to a little girl they had met at a church camp.

The father of the girl happened to be a police officer, and he had been able to trace the calls back to Chuck's house. The officer said he would not press charges if the parents took care of the situation. Chuck's mother wanted us to know, and we were thankful that she had the courage to call us.

We sat down with Alan and talked with him about his behavior and how inappropriate it was. During our discussion with him, we found out that Chuck had access to sites on the Internet that we don't allow our children to see.

That did it! Chuck became off-limits for Alan. We explained why and punished him for his part in the phone calls. We thought that would be the end of it, but it wasn't. The incident began a series of problems that went on for almost a year. Alan didn't want to give up his friendship with Chuck because he liked Chuck's boldness, humor, and defiant attitude, which he began to emulate.

Alan's whole demeanor changed. He began getting in trouble at school for being disrespectful. He had never done that before, and we knew it was Chuck's influence. We thought about pulling Alan out of the school, but he needed the academic environment and help that this small Christian school could give him. He was able to be a major player on a sports team, and we didn't want him to lose that opportunity. Besides, we didn't want to teach him that when things get tough, you just bail out. We know that Alan will come across "bad" people throughout the rest of his life. He had to learn to deal with the situation, and we wanted him to develop the courage and wisdom to let Chuck go.

The whole process was a real battle. Alan was grounded off and on for over a year—cut off from the phone, the television, and doing overnights with friends. Twice we even sent him to a Saturday sheriff's boot camp. It helped some, but not totally.

Alan saw Chuck at school every day. He played on the same sports teams. But they were not allowed to socialize outside of school, and for a time the principal saw to it that they were separated during the school day. Alan was not allowed to call Chuck, and Chuck was not allowed to call our house. Alan knew that if we caught him spending time with Chuck, he would be grounded yet again…and longer.

It is tough, grounding a child for a year, but we refused to give up on Alan, and thankfully, we eventually saw some reasons to be encouraged.

We want Alan to learn that the people he chooses to hang around with can influence his life for good or for bad. Of course parents want their children to choose the good. Sometimes, though, it takes a few hard lessons to get them pointed in the right direction.

One action we took to help Alan see how good he has it was to send him to Brazil, his home country. He spent the summer before his senior year of high school touring with a family friend who works in orphanages there. His eyes definitely began to open.

It has been a struggle with Alan, but we know it will be well worth it in the long run. We can't and won't give up.

CAREER

When we see that one of our children has definite skills and strengths in a particular area, we try to encourage her and provide opportunities for growth in that area. We've never told any of our children what they should be when they grow up. But we do what we can to get them headed in a direction that's right for them.

We want our children to be happy and to have the satisfaction of knowing that they're making a positive contribution to the world. It would be truly horrible to spend forty or more years of your life stuck in a job you hated, and we don't want that to happen to any of our children.

That's another reason why we encourage them to get involved in projects at school and after school. We want them to be willing to take risks and to try something new every once in a while. No matter how young your children may be, someday they'll choose a career, and the seeds you plant today may help them choose wisely.

DRUGS AND ALCOHOL

When I (Pat) was a kid, illegal drugs were called 'dope.' Anyone who was addicted to drugs was called a 'dope fiend.' I'm glad we're a bit more compassionate now, but I liked the term *dope* because it reminded me that that's what you had to be to get hooked on things like cocaine, heroin, or speed.

In Deuteronomy 18:10, God says, "Let no one be found among you who…practices divination or sorcery." The word translated into English as "sorcery" is also the root of the English word *pharmaceuticals*—in other words, drugs or narcotics.

What's our point? Drugs can take control of a person's life as surely as if he were under a powerful spell. They lead to spiritual darkness and destruction. When laboratory monkeys were forced to choose between cocaine and food, they chose cocaine. Some of them did so until they starved to death. Such is the nature of the choke hold drugs can get on a person's life.

As for alcohol, the television commercials make it look cool, and if there's anything children want to be, it's cool. As parents we need to make sure our children know that alcohol does not make you cool. It impairs your judgment, slurs your speech, slows your reflexes, and can cause you to act like a complete fool. Nobody is saying that you will end up as a hopeless wino just because you take a drink or two. But then again that wino didn't start out planning to wear the same clothes for a week, sleep in doorways, and spend his days staggering around in a drunken stupor.

Here are some important facts parents ought to know about alcohol and drugs:

- Alcohol is the most abused drug in the world.
- In the United States the average age when people start drinking is 12.9 years.
- Every year more people between the ages of fifteen and twenty-four die from automobile crashes related to drinking than from any other cause.
- Over 80 percent of all high-school seniors have used alcohol.
- Over half of all high-school seniors say they have been drunk at least once.
- One out of four eighth-graders has been drunk at least once.

- One in four high-school students drinks with a frequency that indicates a problem.
- One in four children in the United States lives in a home where someone is dependent upon alcohol or drugs.
- Nearly half (48 percent) of high-school seniors admit to having used illicit drugs at least once.

A long time ago people used to say, "What you don't know can't hurt you." These days it's just the opposite. What you don't know *can* hurt you and your children. We must be aware of the dangers lurking out there so we can help our children avoid them. Not only must we be aware of the dangers, but we must communicate what we know to our children.

TOBACCO

Another killer is tobacco. Neither Pat nor I (Ruth) have ever smoked a cigarette or any other tobacco product. Why? Several reasons. Pat decided early in his young life that he couldn't be a really good athlete if he smoked. So he didn't.

I decided against smoking for different reasons. I was born with a defective heart, and at the age of twelve, I had open-heart surgery to correct a valve problem. At the time it was an experimental and very dangerous surgery. However, not having the surgery would have meant certain death by the age of twenty-one. As I was leaving the hospital after my surgery, I was on the elevator with my surgeon, and he gave me this piece of advice: "Ruth, I'm only going to tell you one thing. Don't ever smoke. If you do, you'll be back here someday, on the table again." That surgery was the most painful thing in my life, and I certainly didn't want to go through it again. But there is also another reason I stayed away. It's simply that we women spend a lot of money on perfume and bath oils to smell good. Cigarette smoke kills it. So if the health angle doesn't seem to get through to some people, I always go for the smell-good angle. Sometimes image wins over health. Try it. It may work on your daughter or son.

Every child should know that tobacco:

- causes all sorts of diseases, many of them deadly
- gives you a hacking cough that won't go away
- is addicting
- stinks
- turns your teeth yellow
- gives you bad breath
- burns holes in your clothes and furniture

Just before this book went to press we read this powerful information presented by an Australian author, Dr. John Tickell:

You smoke?

You're kidding me.

The stuff that comes out of the back end of a cigarette is basically the same stuff that comes out the back end of an automobile. Carbon monoxide, hydrogen cyanide—they are lethal poisons. And people worry about chemical threats!

There are two relevant statements regarding cigarette smoking.

Statement No. 1: IT IS IMPOSSIBLE TO BE INTELLIGENT AND SMOKE AT THE SAME TIME.

Statement No. 2: THE AVERAGE SMOKER SMOKES TWENTY CIGARETTES A DAY FOR THIRTY-FIVE YEARS. THAT'S A QUARTER OF A MILLION CIGARETTES.

Now that's not a group of people, that's each average smoker—two hundred and fifty thousand cigarettes, and there's ten puffs in every cigarette.

People do it to themselves. Unbelievable, isn't it?

Unbelievable!

P.S. If your lungs were on the outside (instead of on the inside), where you could actually see them, no one, but no one, would smoke.

That's why we teach our children very early on about the dangerous weed called tobacco.

DIET

More than half of all Americans are overweight, and being overweight causes all kinds of health problems. That's why we parents need to teach our children the importance of a healthy diet. The eating habits they develop now will most likely stay with them the rest of their lives. In other words, too many doughnuts, french fries, red meat, and fried foods now may hurt your kids later on.

But we don't make mealtime a battleground. We don't insist that our children "clean their plates," nor do we tell them that they have to eat all their vegetables before they can have dessert. Our goal is always to make our time together (on the rare occasions when we can all get together!) as pleasant as possible for everyone. And we do encourage our children to eat properly. We keep things like grapes, carrots, and nuts on hand for snacking, and we limit access to things like chips and candy.

Everyone has choices. The choices we make—and the choices we help our sons and daughters make—can impact our children's lives forever. As Henry Ward Beecher wrote, "What the mother sings to the cradle, goes all the way down to the coffin."

Chapter 7

Helping Your Children Develop a Sense of Wonder

We have not completely fulfilled our responsibility as parents until we bequeath to our children a love of books, a thirst for knowledge, a hunger for righteousness, an awareness of beauty, a memory of kindness, an understanding of loyalty, a vision of greatness, and a good name.

William Arthur Ward

Ever had a conversation like this?

"Come on, honey, eat a little bit of your spinach."

"But I don't like spinach!"

"How do you know? Come on, just taste it!"

"No! It's yucky!"

"But how do you know if you won't even try it?"

"I just know. I don't like it!"

Most parents have had at least one such conversation and probably many more. We hear those last four words—"I don't like it!"—about a lot of things: math, reading, classical music, the theater, church, visiting the art museum, and so on.

But it is our job as parents to expose our children to a smorgasbord of experiences—whether or not they want to sample them. But in doing so we can help open our children's eyes to the many wonderful experiences God's creation has to offer and instill in them a sense of wonder regarding the gifts he has given us.

INTRODUCING A WORLD OF WONDER

In his book *The Ragamuffin Gospel,* Brennan Manning tells the story of a rabbi named Abraham Joshua Heschel. When Heschel was in the hospital after a near-fatal heart attack, he told a friend, "Sam, I feel only gratitude for my life, for every moment I have lived. I am ready to go. I have seen so many miracles during my lifetime." After a long pause he continued, "Sam, never once in my life did I ask God for wisdom or power or fame. I asked for wonder and he gave it to me."

Manning goes on to decry the fact that so many people have lost their sense of wonder. He says: "By and large, our world has lost its sense of wonder. We have grown up. We no longer catch our breath at the sight of a rainbow or the scent of a rose, as we once did. We have grown bigger and everything else smaller, less impressive. We get blasé, worldly wise, and sophisticated. We no longer run our fingers through water, no longer shout at the stars or make faces at the moon."

Pablo Casals, the brilliant cellist, said something very similar: "Each second we live is a new and unique moment of the universe, a moment that will never be lived again. And what do we teach our children? We teach them that two and two make four and that Paris is the capital of France. When will we also teach them what they are? We should say to each of them: 'Do you know what you are? You are a marvel. You are unique. In all the years that have passed, there has never been a child like you: your legs, your arms, your clever fingers, the way you move. You may become a Shakespeare, a Michelangelo, a Beethoven. You have the capacity for anything. Yes, you are a marvel!' "

We parents have the vitally important job of opening our children's eyes and hearts to the wonders that surround them. As Manning writes: "Our world is saturated with grace, and the lurking presence of God is revealed not only in spirit but in matter—in a deer leaping across a meadow, in the flight of an eagle, in fire and water, in a rainbow after a summer storm, in a gentle doe streaking through a forest, in Beethoven's Ninth Symphony, in a child licking a chocolate ice-cream cone, in a woman with windblown hair. God intended for us to discover His loving presence in the world around us."

There is so much goodness to experience if we'll just be open to it! I (Pat) grew up in a house of sports nuts. Dad was a coach and gave me my first baseball glove when I was three. Mom was as big a baseball fan as Dad, maybe even bigger. Mom and Dad both used to play ball with me in the backyard, and Dad took me to my first major league game when I was seven.

But I also learned early on that there is more to life than baseball. Mom exposed me to many cultural influences. She was a fanatic about reading, and she continually read aloud to me when I was a little boy. That's why I've been a compulsive reader all my life, reading three to five books a week. Music and the arts were also a big part of our family life. We often went to New York and Philadelphia to visit museums, attend concerts, go to the zoo, and see Broadway shows. I didn't have a lot of musical talent, but to this day I can enjoy and discuss Gilbert and Sullivan and the whole Broadway scene.

We try to raise our children in the same well-rounded way. We expose each child to a variety of experiences. Eventually at least one of those experiences clicks and opens a whole new world for that child—we hope.

Our son Alan arrived from Brazil in 1993 at the age of eight. We immediately got him into a routine of school, chores, spiritual instruction, and sports. The first basketball game he ever saw was a game he played in, so his approach was a bit unusual—a potpourri of volleyball, soccer, football, and wrestling, plus a little dribbling and shooting.

At one point in the game, Alan got hold of the ball and he sort of dribbled-ran-drop-kicked it toward the basket. Well, by some miracle known only to the angels, the ball slid right through the net. Alan was one ecstatic eight-year-old. After the game he was talking about a hundred miles an hour in Portuguese, repeating over and over a phrase that sounded like "Quasi Michael Jordan." He was saying, "I'm almost Michael Jordan!"

Wow! Just a few weeks earlier that little tyke had been running through the streets of São Paulo with no future and no concept of the big, wide world beyond his gritty, grimy restricted horizon. Suddenly he had a moment of glory and saw himself soaring with Air Jordan.

We tell you this story because it represents the types of things we parents need to do with all of our kids, which is to expose them to experiences, challenges, and influences that will widen their horizons and inspire dreams of an exciting, incredible future.

ENCOURAGING A SPIRIT OF ADVENTURE

We have discovered that it is very important for parents to encourage their children's sense of adventure. Because we know that little children need protection, it's easy to go overboard in that direction. We constantly tell them what not to do:

- "*Don't* cross the street without looking both ways."
- "*Don't* go near the swimming pool when there's no adult around."
- "*Don't* play with matches."
- "*Don't* take candy from strangers."
- "*Don't* ride your bike in the street."

Although teaching our children how to stay out of danger is certainly important, we need to balance that with encouraging them to explore and experience the world. Too much negativity can instill unnecessary fear and leave our children afraid to try anything new.

Eleanor Roosevelt once said, "There is a wonderful word—Why?—that children, all children, use. When they stop using it, the reason, too often, is that no one bothered to answer them. No one focused and cultivated the child's innate sense of the adventure of life." Mrs. Roosevelt also said, "I think, at a child's birth, if a mother could ask a fairy godmother to endow it with the most useful gift, that gift would be curiosity."

She also urged parents to "stop shielding your children and clipping their wings. Allow your children to develop along their own lines. Don't prevent self-reliance and initiative. The next generation will take care of itself."

Orville Wright, who, along with his brother Wilbur, invented the airplane, credited his parents with encouraging his spirit of adventure. He said that he and his brother "were lucky enough to grow up in an environment where there was always much encouragement to children to pursue intellectual interests, to investigate whatever aroused curiosity." Had that not been the case, we would probably not know the Wright Brothers' names today.

Condoleezza Rice, who has been such an important and influential member of President George W. Bush's cabinet, also grew up in a home where adventure was encouraged. Author Antonia Felix says that her parents "showered their daughter with love, attention, praise, and exposure to all the elements of Western culture—music, ballet, foreign language, athletics, and the great books. 'I had parents who gave me every conceivable opportunity,' she [Condoleezza] said. 'They believed in achievement.' "

We discovered a long time ago that good things happen when parents take their children's questions seriously and help them find the answers they're seeking.

"Why is the sky blue, Mommy?"

"I'm not sure. Why don't we go to the library and see what we can find out?"

We realize that this may sound idealistic. You can't always drop what you're doing and try to find answers to your children's questions. But sometimes you can. And when you do, you'll encourage your children to seek and explore on their own.

Dr. Gordon MacDonald believes that parents should be on the lookout for what he calls "teachable moments." He writes, "We rarely create them; rather we sense them. The intellect of a child has doors like the entryways of a building. A teachable moment happens when that door has, through some circumstances, been thrown open. Parents learn that the signals of a teachable moment vary with each child. For some, the signal is seen in a wistful look on the face; for others, it begins with certain types of questions. Don't overlook the 'captive-audience' moments at the dinner table, driving in the car, in the relaxed evenings, and in those most significant moments just before bedtime."

David Hartman, actor and former host of *Good Morning America*, told *Parade* magazine that his parents always encouraged him to try new things. "They taught me that failure wasn't wrong, that it was the lack of trying that was bad." Thus, by the time Hartman was sixteen, "I played lots of sports, six musical instruments, wrote for the school newspaper, and sang in the school choral group. He (my father) took me on business trips (my parents' way of showing me the world from their shoulders). It was lovely and I've never forgotten it."

He added, "It was this special contact with my parents that made life so alive."

THE RED THREAD

Writer Claire Safran asks, "What makes an Einstein? A Van Cliburn? A Chris Evert Lloyd? Great talent has always been a mystery. Where does it come from? How does it grow?" She goes on to tell of a five-year study undertaken by researcher Benjamin Bloom and a team of assistants from the University of Chicago. The study evaluated the childhoods of 120 superstars from various fields, "the best and the brightest, the tops in their fields."

Safran says, "Surprisingly, the educational detectives found that such superstars aren't simply born—they are brought up that way. Their talents may differ, but their childhood experiences tend to be remarkably similar. If Bloom is right—and many leading educators believe he is—then potential talent is more common than we think. Indeed, Bloom feels that the great majority of children, given the right conditions, can learn almost anything. 'Human potential,' he insists, 'is much greater than we can measure in I.Q. or aptitude tests.' "

Bloom came to this conclusion after interviewing not only the superachievers themselves but their parents as well. He warns that these parents did not set out with the idea of turning their children into heroes. "If you set out to raise a great talent, you probably won't succeed, because you'll push too hard," he said. The parents of the 120 people in Bloom's study simply did what they thought was best for their children at the time.

One mother recalls taking her son on frequent visits to the art museum. He grew up to be a well-known sculptor.

A tennis player's mother says she sat her daughter's car seat by the court while she played the sport. "The ping of tennis balls may be the first sound my daughter remembers hearing," she says.

When you encourage your children in any field, you never know what will happen. For example, when she was a girl, Ruth spent quite a bit of time watching sports on television with her father and little brother. Because she had a heart condition, she was not able to play sports, but she learned to love a variety of athletic events—especially college football.

In my (Ruth) early thirties (after having had heart surgery at age twelve), I decided to take tennis lessons. I had never done anything athletic in my life, but tennis appealed to me. As it turned out, I was good at it. In fact, I won several country club championships.

While I was learning the game, Stephanie, my oldest, was a little girl, so I took her with me to the court when I played or practiced. Several other mothers did the same thing. Stephanie enjoyed watching me play and, at the age of eight, decided that she wanted to take lessons.

I encouraged her in that interest and quickly discovered that she was very good at the sport. So good, in fact, that when she was a freshman in high school, she played on the varsity team. She played all through high school, and in her senior year several small colleges made scholarship offers. She turned them down because she wanted to stay close to home and attend the University of Florida.

At the university she started out majoring in journalism. But one day, during her sophomore year, she came home with the news that she was thinking about switching her major to an exciting new program she had just heard about: sports management.

She asked me what I thought, and I said, "Go for it."

She did, and she has spent her career doing what she loves—working in sports. It all started with her watching me play tennis, then I encouraged her interest in the sport, and it developed into a career. Claire Safran writes, "In almost all the cases, that's how the twig was bent. The child tried the activity his parents seemed to enjoy."

As for Dr. Bloom, he says, "If there's music in a home, that doesn't mean the child will become a musician. But if there's no music in the home, he probably won't." He also found that children often chose the activities their parents encouraged over activities their parents ignored. Pat has firsthand evidence that what Dr. Bloom is saying is true.

I (Pat) have not been a perfect parent. I haven't batted a thousand with my kids. And like anyone else, I have a tendency to look back and see some areas where I've made mistakes. But I learned a long time ago that it doesn't do any good to look back. All you can do is learn from your mistakes and keep on moving forward.

One thing I do know is that when it comes to showing love to my children or disciplining them, I have tried to treat them all the same. But what has worked with some of them has not worked with others. Bobby, my second son, is one of those cases where everything seemed to go right.

Bobby is a perfect example of what I've heard called "the red thread" theory. Basically, this idea says that children have a red thread running through their lives—a thread that represents their passions, interests, and skills. The parents' job is to look for that thread and encourage their children's development in those areas, whatever they may be.

It was clear to me from the time he was a very little boy that Bobby was interested in baseball. This was true even though I was employed by a professional basketball team: the Philadelphia 76ers. Bobby *liked* basketball, but he *loved* baseball. Because he loved baseball so much, I often took him and his older brother, Jimmy, to Veterans Stadium to see the Phillies play. He was thrilled whenever I'd get a field pass so we could go down and visit with players like Mike Schmidt and Bob Boone.

Then, when Bobby was nine, we moved to Florida where the weather is good enough to play baseball all year round. And that's pretty much what he did. When he wasn't playing baseball, watching it on television, or talking about it, he was working as a bat boy for a Minnesota Twins minor league franchise, which was based in Orlando at the time.

He went on to an outstanding high-school career as a catcher (my position in high school and college) and then played at Rollins College. Even though Bobby was a good player, he knew he wasn't going to make it to the big leagues, so upon graduating from Rollins, he got an internship with the Cincinnati Reds. Soon after that his internship turned into a full-time coaching job. Now in his late twenties, I believe he has a tremendous career ahead of him in the sport.

It pleases me that I have a great relationship with Bobby and that he always seeks my counsel about important decisions. Of course I'm proud of the way things have turned out for Bobby. But I wonder if any of this would have happened without all those evenings together at the Vet, nearly twenty years ago now, watching the Phillies play baseball.

Whether you like spending a leisurely afternoon in an art museum, enjoying an evening at the symphony, or taking in a football game at the local university, chances are very good that your parents had something to do with it. If you participate in and enjoy many of the things we've mentioned, you should probably thank your parents for helping you become a well-rounded person, then determine that you'll do the same thing for your kids.

By the way, even though experience has taught us that early exposure to culture helps to create a healthy interest, we've also seen that this is not an absolute necessity. Some of our children were approaching adolescence when we adopted them. They had never had the opportunity or the time to read a book. All their time had been spent just trying to survive. But once they discovered the joy of reading, they quickly made up for lost time.

DIP INTO THE MELTING POT

We mentioned in chapter 2 that dinner in the Williams household often resembles a meeting of the United Nations General Assembly because so many different cultures and nationalities are represented. We can't imagine having it any other way. We have learned so much from our children's different perspectives on life.

One of the great strengths of the United States has always been our "melting pot" personality. We are privileged to live in a country where so many nationalities and ethnic groups are represented. We believe that cultural diversity comes from God. That we are so different from each other is an indication of God's creativity and artistry, as is the fact that there are so many different types and colors of birds, animals, and plants. God is not monotonous. He uses all the colors in his palette!

We are blessed in the United States that immigrants from Germany gave us the polka, sauerkraut, and Wiener schnitzel. Americans who came from Mexico brought us tacos and enchiladas, mariachi music, and the archways, fountains, and plazas that are such an important part of Southwestern architecture. Where would we be without our friends from Italy who gave us opera, pasta, pizza, and so many beautiful paintings and sculptures?

We could go on and on about the benefits that have come to American society from cultures and countries all over the world—from Africa, Asia, South America. Every culture has its own music, architecture, food, clothing, colors, and styles.

Again, we believe this diversity is God-ordained and something he put here for our enjoyment and edification. In a way, these different cultures represent various facets of God's personality. By encouraging our children to appreciate and understand these differences, we are encouraging them to have a better understanding of who God is.

If you've been around since the seventies, you might remember the old Alka-Seltzer advertising line, "Try it! You'll like it!" Children in America are surrounded by opportunities to learn all the best things the world's various cultures have to offer. We have to be the ones to encourage them to try new things—things that might even sound bizarre to them, like opera! If they try it, they might like it, and it might help them to grow into well-rounded, well-educated adults.

One evening we took the kids to eat at The Cheesecake Factory. I (Ruth) love fried calamari and ordered it as an appetizer. Kati, one of our more adventurous children, asked what it was. I gave her a mysterious look and said, "Just try it."

As she took the big step of putting it in her mouth, I asked, "Kati, do you know what you're eating?"

"No," she replied.

"Squid."

As soon as the word was out of my mouth, the calamari was out of Kati's mouth.

I said later, "I shouldn't have spoken so soon. She probably would have liked it."

That's an important lesson: Don't tell your children what they're eating until they've swallowed it. Or, better yet, don't ever tell them what it is, and they'll grow up loving it!

One more story about Kati before we move on. Kati loves music, but her piano teachers all became discouraged with her because she didn't want to practice published music. She prefers to play her own "compositions." So we gave up on piano lessons several years ago.

What made Kati's music even more difficult for us to bear was the fact that we had an old piano that was badly in need of tuning (not to mention other needed repairs). Mozart wouldn't have sounded very good on that piano. And Kati drove everyone in the house crazy, playing her "music" on that thing. Finally we decided that we just couldn't take it anymore and got rid of the piano.

But at Christmas two years ago, Santa Claus brought Kati an electronic keyboard that she could keep in her room—and the very best thing about it is that it came with headphones. (That Santa is a pretty smart fellow!)

Now she composes and plays her own music in the privacy of her room. She's even recorded some CDs for us to listen to, and she's becoming quite good. We can see that Kati's musical explorations are paying off. We're happy that we found a way for Kati to go through her musical growing pains without the rest of us suffering through them with her.

Who knows if anything will ever come of Kati's music? That doesn't even matter. What matters most is that she is doing what she loves: composing music.

We believe that music will continue to be a big part of Kati's life. She just needed to be able to do it her way. It was simply a matter of encouraging her and giving her the opportunity to find out what she could do.

ENCOURAGE YOUR CHILD'S STRENGTHS

Another way to encourage your children's sense of wonder and adventure is to find out what their natural aptitudes and desires are, then encourage them in those areas.

In his bestseller *Seven Habits of Highly Effective People,* Dr. Steven R. Covey tells about a friend whose son was crazy about baseball. "My friend wasn't interested in baseball at all," Covey writes, "but one summer he took his son to see every major league team play one game."

Covey says that it took over six weeks for them to make the trip to various ballparks around the country and "cost a great deal of money, but it became a powerful bonding experience in their relationship. My friend was asked, on his return, 'Do you like baseball that much?' 'No,' he replied, 'but I like my son that much.' "

Earlier we mentioned a study by Benjamin Bloom in which he and his team of researchers from the University of Chicago discovered the supreme importance of a parent's encouragement in helping a child grow into a successful adult. Bloom quotes a gold medal–winning Olympic athlete as saying, "My father taught me that if a thing is worth doing, it's worth doing well." Almost all the other successful people interviewed in Bloom's study had similar encouragement from their parents.

Bloom also found that success did not come easily or overnight for any of the 120 superachievers included in the study. None of them were prodigies. Not one of them just sat down at the piano and started playing like Mozart when they were three years old. Nobody was solving complicated algebraic equations in his crib. Instead, according to Claire Safran, "The parents in this study tried to give their children the experiences that seemed right for them at each stage." Here's what they did:

- *Parents put their children's development first.* Almost without exception, the parents in Dr. Bloom's study made sacrifices to provide lessons, equipment, and other help for their children. The father of a young musician spent money on a grand piano instead of a new car. The family of a tennis star spent weekends taking their daughter to junior tournaments. Parents often put off meeting their own needs and desires in order to help their children succeed. (And what parent isn't familiar with sacrifice?)

- *The parents were quick to encourage and not so quick to criticize.* Safran writes: "If a future star grew discouraged, the parents offered encouragement. When a young swimmer moved into a new age group and found himself losing every race, he wanted to quit. His father told him, 'Just hang on until you win one more time. Don't quit simply because you're losing.' By the time he won again, the boy wanted to go on. The parents cheered them when they won and comforted them when they lost. If a child tried hard or did better than the last time, that, too, was a victory. Or a loss could be something to learn from, a way of seeing what you needed to work on. After a while, though, it was up to the child."

- *At an early age, almost all the children were given lessons to develop their talent.* The teachers the parents chose were not necessarily the best in their fields. They were chosen as much for their ability to relate to children as they were for their own talent. These men and women possessed warm, friendly personalities and were quick to praise their pupils' efforts.

- *They were asked to keep at it until they got it right.* When the parents felt their children had gone about as far as they could go under their initial instructors, they brought in teachers who were more demanding. The student was made to keep working on a tennis stroke, a piece of classical music, or a painting until she got it absolutely right. Perseverance was the key in this period of the child's development; parents adhered to the belief that practice does indeed make perfect.

- *A master teacher was hired.* In the final stages of a child's development a master teacher was brought in, someone who, according to Claire Safran, was "both master and role model—an outstanding trainer of outstanding talent."

According to Dr. Bloom's research, by the time the people in his study entered their teen years, they were devoting an average of twenty-five hours a week to their chosen field. That was more than they spent on any other activity, including school. But as writer Safran points out, it is no more time than the average child spends sitting in front of a television or DVD player.

And while we're on the subject of television, we should point out that watching television is what the average child does most during his waking hours—and that's not good. The American Academy of Pediatrics' Task Force on Children and Television has stated that repeated exposure to television violence can make children more accepting of real-life violence and more violent themselves. Certainly any good parents would want to help their kids find the good things on television—the educational, the motivational, and the challenging. But children's television watching should be closely monitored. As one law enforcement official we know said, "Today's children spend most of their time in a high-crime area: in front of the television set."

It's important to note that the superachieving children studied were *not* made to spend every waking hour at the piano, on the tennis court, in the swimming pool, or solving math problems. They worked hard, yes, but they were not pushed to the point of becoming frustrated and angry. In fact, some of the parents in the study said they had other children who were more talented, but they chose not to work as hard at developing their skills as their supersuccessful siblings did.

One special note: Dr. Bloom's study found that while most of the superstar parents enjoyed and encouraged their children's talents, they were not living their own lives vicariously through their child's accomplishments. They didn't base their own self-esteem on their child's victories, nor were they embarrassed and humiliated when their child failed in some way. They knew that the successes being achieved were their child's, not their own.

Before going on to a discussion about discipline, we thought you might enjoy a humor break. These "Great Truths About Life" were collected from the experiences of real children:

- No matter how hard you try, you can't baptize cats.
- Never let your mom brush your hair when she's mad at your dad.
- If your sister hits you, don't hit her back. Parents always catch the second person.
- Never ask your three-year-old brother to hold a tomato.
- You can't trust dogs to guard your food.
- Don't sneeze when someone is cutting your hair.
- Puppies still have bad breath even after you give them a tic tac.
- Never try to hold a vacuum cleaner and a cat at the same time.
- You can't hide a piece of broccoli in a glass of milk.
- You shouldn't wear polka-dot underwear underneath white shorts.
- The best place to be when you are sad is in Grandma's lap.

PART FOUR

The Blessings and Burdens
of Love and Discipline

Chapter 8

Tough Love for Tough Times

Your children need a parent, not a pal. You better be a parent if you ever want to earn the right to be a pal.

Jay Strack

One morning when I (Ruth) was working in my office at home, I received a phone call from Alan's school. Alan, who was thirteen years old at the time, was giving one of his teachers a hard time. He had refused to complete a particular assignment and had been disrespectful. As a result he was going to be kept after school for an hour.

We had been having the same type of problem with Alan at home. He always felt that he knew what was best for him (so typical of thirteen-year-olds). He didn't want his teachers or his parents telling him how to behave.

We told him that we were going to ground him for two weeks, and he really blew a gasket! "It's not fair!" he whined. "No one else gets in trouble at school *and* at home! I hate living here. I want to move out!"

"But, Alan," I asked, "where would you go?"

"I can live on the street," he shot back. "I did it in Brazil. I can do it here."

"But how would you eat? Where would you sleep?" While he was thinking about those questions, I gave him a few more things to consider. "What about your PlayStation 2? Your video games? Your basketball hoop?"

"I don't need all this stuff. I don't even want it."

He went on to assure me that he'd be just fine sleeping on the streets. "I don't need you or Dad to support me!"

I sighed and slowly shook my head.

"Alan, why don't you sleep on it? You can decide tomorrow. However, if you decide to stay, you'll be grounded for two weeks." I also told him, "Dad and I love you very much. We're trying to help you learn to be respectful and follow the rules at school." Then I gave him a hug and a kiss.

The next morning, while Alan was at school, our house manager, Angel Garcia, and I acted on Alan's statement and moved all of his furniture and clothes out of his room—except for his alarm clock and a few changes of underwear to go with his school uniforms.

As you can imagine, Alan was shocked when he came home from school and discovered that his room was empty. "What happened to all my stuff?" he demanded.

"Well, Alan," I replied, "you said you didn't want it, so we got rid of it." Looking around at all the empty space, I said, "It will sure be easier to clean this way. Oh, by the way, the television is off-limits. Also, don't use the phone. You can come downstairs to eat dinner, but otherwise just stay in your room."

I went on, "Please let us know what you plan to do in the future. If you decide to leave, I'll help you pack your clothes, but that's all you can take. Everything else stays here."

"But where will I do my homework?"

"On the floor, I guess."

"Where do I sleep?"

"Same place."

"Do I get a pillow?"

"No."

Believe me, this was one of the hardest things I have ever done. Alan is my baby. He was devastated, and I was dying inside. At bedtime I went upstairs and gave him a hug and a kiss. So did Pat. The other kids were dumbfounded. "Are you really going to let him leave?" they asked. I don't think any of us got any sleep that night.

The next day, I returned from a speaking engagement to find a handwritten note slipped underneath the master bedroom door. It read:

Mom and Dad,

I am so sorry for how I acted yesterday. I don't know why I said I wanted to move out of the house. If I was to move out of the house, I would be dead without you. None of this would have happened if I would have just been good at school. You always know what you are doing, and you guys are always right. I hope that you can forgive me for all of the trouble I have been. I am not saying all of this so I can get my room, video games, clothes, and other stuff back. I hope that this won't end our relationship.

     Love,

     Alan

P.S. I promise that I am going to work very hard. Please come up to talk to me.

Of course Pat and I both went up to talk to Alan. Then we took a walk around the block with him and explained how hard it was to discipline him, but that discipline was necessary to help him grow up to become a good human being. He spent one more night on the floor, and the next day we moved everything back into his room. He was grounded for two weeks.

We've never been afraid to discipline our children when they needed it—and it seems someone has needed it almost every day. Honestly, there have been plenty of times when we thought that everything we told our kids went in one ear and came right out the other with no sign that it was being slowed down by anything in between!

We know that some parents hesitate to discipline their children because they're afraid their children will hate them. That has not been an issue for us. Instead we've sometimes been tempted to go easy on one of our children because he spent the first few years of his life in terrible poverty. We are inclined to think, "Oh, he's suffered enough." But then we remind ourselves that firm, loving discipline is a vital part of helping our children develop their God-given potential. Without it, their lives may become a mess.

TO SPANK OR NOT TO SPANK?

One day when I (Ruth) was in a child psychology class at Rollins College working on my master's degree in psychology, the discussion turned to discipline. The professor wanted to know which forms of discipline students felt were appropriate and which were inappropriate.

"What about spanking?" she asked. "How do you feel about that?"

Everyone in the class thought it was wrong, except for me and one other member of the class.

The other students were appalled. "How could you ever spank a child?" one of them asked. "That's child abuse."

I laughed and responded, "My mother spanked me. In fact, she kept a paddle on top of the refrigerator. Sometimes all she had to do was pretend to reach for it, and my brother and I straightened out real quick."

"But that's using fear," someone said.

"Right," I responded, "and it worked. I turned out pretty well, and so did my brother. Also, I spank my kids and they're okay."

The truth is that without spanking, parents don't have much control over some children. And for children to learn respect for superiors, they have to know who's in charge. Children have many different personalities. With some of them, talking works. With others, talking doesn't do a thing, and a swat or two on the bottom is necessary to get their attention. (We just heard about a new study that claims spanking is bad for children. However, experts are suspicious because the whole study is written in crayon!)

Our good friend Bobby Malkmus, who once played for the Phillies, Braves, and Senators, tells us about the time, nearly forty years ago, when his six-year-old son James acted up in church. After speaking to him twice without getting any results, Bobby finally told the boy, "When we get home, you're going to get a spanking." Bobby remembers, "This was the hardest thing I ever had to do. When we got home, I took James to his room and, before spanking him, told him that it was going to hurt me more than it would hurt him.

I don't think he believed me. After I spanked him, I took him into my arms and told him I loved him."

Bobby continues, "A couple of years ago, I asked my son, who is now forty-five, what he remembers most about growing up. He said the time I took him to his room after church and spanked him!"

James remembers that incident because it had a profound effect on his behavior. It impressed upon him the importance of behaving properly and respecting authority, teaching an important lesson that has stayed with him throughout his life.

A few years later, when James was a teenager, he played on a baseball team that scheduled several games for Sunday morning. Even though Bobby and his wife, Ruth, did not try to influence their son's decision, the boy went to his coach and said he would not be able to play in any game that got in the way of his going to church. The firm, loving discipline his parents gave him when he was a child had helped him get life's priorities in the proper order.

Flowers or Weeds?

A story is told about a conversation between poet Samuel Taylor Coleridge and a man who believed that children should be allowed to do whatever they wanted to do whenever they wanted to do it. "I believe children should be given a free rein to think and act," he said, "and thus learn at an early age to make their own decisions. This is the only way they can grow into their full potential."

In reply Coleridge said simply, "Come see my flower garden."

His visitor followed Coleridge to the back of the house, where he was surprised by the sight of an untidy piece of ground without a single flower in it. "Why, that's nothing but a yard full of weeds," he said.

"It used to be filled with roses," Coleridge explained. "But this year I thought I'd let the garden grow as it willed without tending to it. This is the result."

The poet's point was well made. Flower gardens need plenty of tending, and children need even more if they're going to grow into the beautiful, productive adults we want them to be. I (Ruth) often use the following quote in my seminars: "Life is like a garden. You have to weed it regularly if you want it to be beautiful."

Who knows what children may become left untended? The child who is indulged and spoiled may wind up like Frederick, an eighteenth-century prince of Wales. Frederick was described by his mother, Queen Caroline, as "the greatest liar and the greatest canaille and the greatest beast in the whole world." Sorry, Mom. Maybe he needed to have his bottom swatted once or twice when he was a child. Or to be grounded when he disobeyed.

In the 1950s, Roman Catholic Archbishop Fulton Sheen was one of the most popular television personalities in America—so popular, in fact, that he scored a ratings upset over Milton Berle, thus knocking the comedian's variety show off the air. The archbishop once said, "Give me your children until they are seven, and I will mold them for life." In other words, the things children learn when they are very young will stay with them for the rest of their lives. For that reason, it's never too early to teach your children to:

- do the right thing in all situations
- respect and obey those who have been placed in authority over them—most especially you!
- be courteous and polite
- be honest, trustworthy, and fair
- respect the rights of others
- share their toys with the other kids
- play nice

After all, little boys and girls who play nice with others are most likely going to grow into decent, caring adults who work nice at the office. Children who never learn to respect others, share, or play nice may wind up doing things like flying planes into the World Trade Center, killing a dozen people with a sniper's gun in our nation's capital, or going on a shooting spree at their high school, killing fellow students and teachers.

Saddam Hussein, who murdered his own people and pillaged his own country, is a case in point. According to Wes Smith, writing in the *Orlando Sentinel,* when Hussein was a young boy, his stepfather taught him to be a chicken thief. It is alleged that he tortured small animals and that his education ended at age eleven when he shot a teacher. As a teenager he became "a street mugger" for a gang of thugs and then "a low-level political assassin, interrogator, and strong-arm man for his uncle's Baath party."

The rest, as they say, is history. And now, so is he.

Now, of course, Saddam Hussein is far worse than merely an overgrown spoiled brat. But just the same, he was a child once. He had parents who could have molded and guided his character in the right direction. Who knows? He might have used his ambition to bring a better life to the Iraqi people. Instead he became a monster who plunged his country into war. He needed some tough love early on.

We've discovered that for discipline to have a maximum degree of success, it needs to begin very early, as soon as a child begins to understand the difference between right and wrong, yes and no. You can't indulge a child's every whim until he becomes a teenager and then try to crack down on him. In a recent sermon, our pastor, Jim Henry, gave his Four Ds for raising children, and we agree:

1. No disobedience
2. No dishonesty
3. No disrespect
4. No defiance

Having nineteen children has given us plenty of opportunities to analyze the successes and mistakes we have made as parents. One thing we've seen very clearly is that firm, consistent, loving discipline must be a constant presence in a child's life. Jack Stallings, who was Pat's baseball coach at Wake Forest University, once explained the necessary constancy of parental discipline this way: "Parenting is easy. You just do the right thing for the next few minutes. You just straighten this chair and dust that table, and you tell little Johnny to pick up his toys and put them away. That's easy. The hard part is that it never stops!" He added, "You don't have to have a Ph.D. in child psychology to be a good parent. You just have to have a lot of love and an awful lot of patience and persistence!"

WHY DON'T MY KIDS LISTEN TO ME?

One of the most common complaints we hear from other parents is that their kids don't listen to them.

A friend named Rhonda tells us, "I can tell my daughter four or five times to clean up her room, and she acts as if she didn't hear a thing I said. She doesn't even react until I'm screaming at the top of my lungs, and then she says, 'Okay! I hear you! You don't have to yell at me!' "

Craig says his kids never seem to hear him when he calls them to the table for dinner. "They usually come the third time I call them," he said. "Don't ask me why it's so hard to get their attention. I have no idea."

One of the things we've discovered over our years of parenting is that *how* you say something is very important. It's not as important as *what* you say, but it's close.

As parenting expert Renee Grant-Williams writes: "It is the tone in which you say something that makes a big impact on your children. If you allow your voice to rise in a question at the end, it sounds as if you are seeking your child's approval. An order should never sound like a request for agreement or approval. Keep your pitch steady and give finality to your commands. When you become impatient, resist the urge to whine."

Among her other excellent suggestions for parents:

- *Emphasize important words with long consonants.* "Sss-top it nnn-ow" will get better results than whining "St-ah-ah-ah-p," she says.
- *Use an authoritative tone.* "And remember," Grant-Williams says, "if you make everything sound like a crisis, they're likely to ignore you when it really is important."
- *Say what you mean and then stop.* "Children have short attention spans and will tune you out if you ramble on and on. There is a great differ-

ence between commanding, 'Stop it now!' and pleading, 'You kids better stop it right now!' "

- *Bring the volume down.* "Should you find yourself drawn into an intense argument, instead of escalating the volume, you can change the direction of the confrontation by suddenly shifting gears and speaking in a quiet voice.... If one of you lowers your voice, the whole dynamic changes."
- *Say your child's name.* "To get a child to listen to you, try saying his name in a calm, low, well-supported voice that is followed by a long power pause. That pause will get your child's attention; then say what you have to say in a low, steady voice, using plenty of consonants to stress the words you want him to heed."

USE PLENTY OF LOVE

One of my (Ruth) greatest regrets is that I didn't have all the children earlier in their lives. Most of their problems have been the result of the poor conditions they lived in and the abuse they received when they were younger.

On my fiftieth birthday, Pat and the kids threw me a party at home. One of the gifts that I treasure to this day was a box of handwritten notes from the kids. One of the notes came from Thomas, who wrote:

Happy 50th birthday! Well, you're 50, but still going strong. I'm glad you're part of this family, and you're a great mom. I appreciate all that you have done and the loving effort you've put into this family. You're an inspiration and an encourager. You make me a better person. You're a perfect example of what a great mother is, and when I'm 50, I hope to be as kind and generous as you are. My only regret is that you weren't our mom earlier. Thanks for the memories!

Love,

Tom

I have wonderful memories of each child. Some have been easy to raise, some difficult, but I love them all, and I think that one key reason we have had some success with our children is that we have combined lots of love with discipline. We believe very strongly that love without discipline is abuse, just as discipline without love is abuse. The two go hand in hand. Discipline by itself is not abuse. How it's administered and the motive behind it is what makes it abusive. Throwing a child down a flight of stairs because he accidentally broke something is abuse. Punishing a child by taking away his video games for a week is discipline. Scratching a child's face because she won't pick up something she left on the floor is abuse. Swatting a child on the bottom because she talks back to you is discipline. If children aren't disciplined, they won't grow up to be responsible adults. But after being disciplined, children must know they're loved. In fact, they must know that they were disciplined *because* they are loved. There is no love in abuse.

I (Ruth) know from my counseling work that people who abuse children often suffer from very low self-esteem. Because they feel so bad about themselves, they strike out at people who can't fight back. They are control addicts who don't love themselves, and as a result they can't possibly love anyone else. The only way they can continue to have the control they crave is to abuse and manipulate others. The saddest part of this sad story is that unless someone comes along and breaks the chain of abuse, the abused child will probably become an abusive parent. Knowing the abuse that some of our children have experienced, one of our goals as parents has been to show them that there is another, healthy way for parents and children to relate to each other. Hopefully they will choose the healthy role as they grow older and let the unhealthy way go.

WHEN THEY'RE GROWN, LET THEM GO

Before we leave the topic of discipline, we want to point out that once your children are grown and out of the nest, there's not a whole lot you can do to influence their behavior. You are no longer in control of their lives—they are.

A recent story in the *Wall Street Journal* illustrated this point. The headline read, "Williams' Career Takes Wrong Turn." The article went on to tell of Jay Williams, who was selected second in the 2002 NBA draft by the Chicago Bulls. In 2002 Jay's future looked unlimited. In 2003 not only was his career in jeopardy, but doctors questioned whether he would ever again be able to walk normally.

When the *Journal's* story was written, the twenty-one-year-old Williams was in intensive care in a hospital after a horrible motorcycle crash. He had already been through two surgeries and had several more facing him. His accident occurred when he was driving a motorcycle he wasn't licensed to drive. Plus, this joyride was a violation of his NBA contract, which forbade him to ride on motorcycles at all. Everyone in the NBA family hoped Jay's doctors and surgeons could perform miracles and get him back on the court.

This young man made some very bad decisions that could cost him an enviable career. Because we're parents, we were touched by his story. All we could do was shake our heads and sympathize with this young man and his parents.

You see, we've been there. One of our family rules is that we do not buy our kids motorcycles, nor do we want our children riding on one—period. The danger to life and limb, as seen in the Jay Williams story, is very real and always present. But kids don't realize the dangers. They think we're being too protective when we forbid these kinds of things.

Our son Peter, now in his midtwenties, left the Marine Corps to begin training as an underwater welder. Several years ago, right after he completed his basic training, he called us and told us that he needed our help to make a down payment on a motorcycle. We had a long talk with Peter about the dangers of cycling—the same thing we had been telling all the children for years—and advised him to save a little more money so he could buy a used car. We also told him that we felt he should save his own money for a down payment. We wanted him to learn how to make good choices and save money for the things he wants.

Instead, Peter went right out and bought a motorcycle. Several months later we got a call that Peter had crashed his bike and was in the hospital. His left arm was seriously broken and burned and required several surgeries. Peter had to undergo painful physical therapy to regain the use of his arm, which is still badly scarred.

Furthermore, because he didn't have insurance on the motorcycle, he spent several years making payments on a vehicle that had already been destroyed. That was a hard lesson for Peter to learn. Later he told us, "I should have listened to you guys."

I (Ruth) got a note from Peter on my birthday after this incident that said:

> Just want to thank you for your generosity and kindness to me. You
> have been an inspiration to me in everything I do. I just want you to
> know that you are appreciated by me. The reality of disappointing you
> is harsher than the punishment dealt to me.

We parents hope and pray that when our children leave the nest, they will heed the life lessons and follow the good examples we have set for them. But they don't always do that. Peter is one case in point.

Another one of our rules is no tattoos. However, Pat says he will allow one tattoo—with two stipulations. Those stipulations are:

- Pat gets to determine where the tattoo goes: on the forehead.
- He gets to decide what it consists of: big, block letters that say, I AM IN CHARGE OF ME!

I (Pat) have told all my kids that I'll even pay for the tattoo if they'll get one according to my wishes—but so far I've had no takers.

Once our children have moved out of our house, we can no longer insist that they live by our rules. Once they're adults, they make their own decisions. One day recently a couple of our boys who had left high school and moved out on their own came by to visit.

One had his initials tattooed on his arm, and the other had gotten an eyebrow ring. They seemed a little tentative at first, as if they were worried about what our reaction might be. The first thing we did was hug them.

Then we just shook our heads. No sermons. No admonishment. Again, our attitude was, *They are on their own now, so it's their decision.* We certainly don't like what they've done to their bodies, but we certainly do love both of the boys.

One daughter got a tongue ring as soon as she moved out of the house. A year later it was gone, and so was one of her teeth—courtesy of that ring. Now she tells the younger children not to get one. We hope they listen.

We recently saw a teenager who had a ring in her nose, another in her eyebrow, and a stud through her tongue. The poor thing looked like she had fallen face first into someone's tackle box! But some children have to learn the hard way.

Once children leave home, they make their own choices. And sometimes they learn why we have certain rules.

Chapter 9

CARING ENOUGH TO DISCIPLINE

Whoever loves discipline loves knowledge,
but he who hates correction is stupid.
PROVERBS 12:1

Disciplining your children is like walking a tightrope. You don't want to be too lenient, but you don't want to be too strict either. A wrong step in either direction can be disastrous. Here, then, are Ten Commandments of Discipline that we have learned through (sometimes painful) experience:

1. Don't make the mistake of thinking your child ought to have everything he wants.
2. Don't wink at improper behavior and tell yourself, "She's just going through a phase."
3. Make sure that your child knows what you expect of him and that he has a clear understanding of your view of what's right and what's wrong.
4. As much as possible, let your child do things for herself.
5. When he gets into trouble, don't automatically take his side. There are usually at least two points of view to every story.
6. Be understanding, but don't be too quick to make or accept excuses—especially if your child has been giving you a lot of them lately.
7. Make sure he knows that he's not the boss of the family. That position is reserved for Mom and Dad.
8. Don't back down when your child puts you to the test.

9. Stay cool, calm, and collected even when he's pushed all the wrong buttons. Be firm, but not abusive.
10. Discipline your child when she breaks the rules.

1. Don't Think Your Child Ought to Have Everything He Wants

A friend tells us about an incident she recently witnessed in a department store. A mother with her hands full of packages was leaving the store, accompanied by a little boy of three or four.

Placed strategically at the exit was a machine full of big, brightly colored gumballs.

"Mommy!" the little boy shouted. "I want some gum!"

"No, Ralphie. Not this time."

Ralphie pointed at the machine. "I want some gum!"

The first time he spoke, it had sounded like a request. Now it sounded like a demand.

"Mommy has her hands full."

"I want some gum!" This time he screamed.

"I don't have a quarter! Now come on."

Mom was agitated, but so was her little angel. He began to stomp his feet and wail. At that moment, a gumball meant more to that little boy than life itself.

Ralphie's tantrum was attracting the attention of other shoppers. Mom's face was turning red, either from embarrassment or anger—and probably from both.

"Okay! Okay!" she said angrily. She put her bags on the floor, opened her pocketbook, and fumbled through it until she found a quarter. She jammed the money into the machine's coin slot and angrily turned the handle. When an orange gumball emerged, she thrust it into her little boy's hand, gathered up her purchases, and stomped out of the store with her son following her.

Have you ever been there? We have. And we know that it's often a lot easier to give in and allow your child whatever he wants than it is to stand strong and stick to your no. We doubt if there's a parent alive who hasn't overindulged his children at one time or another. We certainly plead guilty. But gumballs quickly give way to other, larger desires and demands. And if we don't draw the line on unreasonable little demands, it will be very hard to stand strong against unreasonable big demands later.

Someone has said, "You don't give children everything they want without also giving them boredom." How true! When a child works for something he really wants, it is more important to him. When he saves his allowance over several weeks to acquire something that is important to him, he will appreciate it more. But when a child knows that anything he wants will be handed to him, he becomes blasé and bored. When that happens, he may seek excitement in other areas, through illegal drugs, illicit sex, or crime.

Not long ago Kati bought a new stereo. Kati loves music, and she has had three stereos—but she has somehow managed to break them all. We told her she'd have to pay for the next one herself. She finally did, spending $212.99 out of $370 she had saved from weeding the yard.

We didn't think this was a good use of her money. But we let Kati do it because it was *her* money. She earned it. After nine months, the stereo is still working. We believe that because she paid for it, she has taken better care of it.

Dr. John Gray, author of *Men Are from Mars, Women Are from Venus,* has also written a book called *Children Are from Heaven.* In it he writes, "It is not giving children more that spoils them. It is giving them more to avoid confrontation."

Giving is good when it's a reward. I (Ruth) must tell you that I love giving. I love spoiling my children, and I guess that's because I learned it from my mother. She spoiled me—in a good way. When I needed her discipline, she gave it…sometimes with the paddle and sometimes by grounding me. But when I was good, she spoiled me by doing things for me and surprising me with thoughtful gifts, and I do the same thing for my children.

When I'm out shopping and see something one of the children would like—and she has been on her best behavior—I buy it, take it home, and place it on her bed. I love to hear the shouts of joy when she goes upstairs and sees what I bought her. What do I buy? Maybe a shirt in a color she likes, or perhaps a CD or a DVD she's been wanting. It doesn't really matter. It may be just a package of chewing gum I know she likes. Whatever it is, the question is always asked, "Why did you get this for me?" That gives me an opportunity to say, "Because you've been so good lately and because I love you."

But parents who indulge their children's every whim simply because they want to avoid a loud or embarrassing confrontation are definitely headed for trouble.

2. DON'T WINK AT IMPROPER BEHAVIOR

When Mom found a pack of cigarettes in her Stacey's school bag, she told herself that her little girl was just "going through a phase." She did the same thing when she discovered that Stacey had gone against her wishes and had a butterfly tattooed on her back. Then came the tongue stud, the pierced eyebrow, and the foul language, all accompanied by frequent outbursts of anger toward her parents.

Then one day Stacey announced defiantly that she was pregnant and that it didn't matter who the father was because she was going to get an abortion. Her parents pleaded with their daughter to reconsider, but legally there was nothing they could do.

Today, at the age of twenty-five, Stacey has had at least three abortions that her parents know about. She lives in a rundown apartment in a crime-infested part of town. She has had a succession of minimum-wage jobs and has been fired from several of them due to her drug and alcohol abuse.

Her parents continue to pray for her, but she refuses to listen to their advice or accept their offers to help her get her life together. She seems content with her squalid lifestyle.

An extreme example? Perhaps. But there are more Staceys than you might expect—children who came from good, solid Christian homes, but who threw it all away. What began as a "phase" catapulted into disaster. All children go through phases, but a phase left unchecked and uncared for will result in a much larger problem. If your child is going through a phase you don't like, our advice is to address it immediately. Talk to your child about it and try to find out why it's happening. Is it a peer thing? Does it have something to do with a boyfriend or girlfriend? Is it just growing pains? Once you've talked things through and discovered what's really going on, you can deal with it properly.

Some rebellious behavior is to be expected. It's part of growing up. It is true that, as youth pastor/editor Wayne Rice writes, "Children need to assert themselves during their adolescent years. They need to separate themselves from their parents and to establish an identity of their own. It's necessary and good for young adolescents to want to act and behave differently than their parents. It's the only way the teen will develop the self-confidence he or she needs to survive, and it's a skill that must be learned through experience."

But he goes on to say, "It is normal for kids to rebel when they become teenagers…[but] rebellion that is harmful and destructive cannot be tolerated, because it is not 'normal.' "

How can you tell the difference between a passing phase and a descent into self-destructive, rebellious behavior? You can't. The best thing we parents can do is enforce the rules we have established for our household and refuse to look the other way when those rules are violated.

The very best way to cut short a negative phase in a child's life is simply to show him that you won't put up with it and that you will hold him to the same high standard you've always set for him—which leads us to the next commandment:

3. Make Sure Your Child Knows What You Expect of Him and Has a Clear Understanding of Right and Wrong

Most of our adopted children were held back a year when they started school in America because they needed to learn English. Besides, most of them hadn't had much formal schooling in their native countries, so they had quite a bit of catching up to do. For that reason they have always been a year older than most of their classmates.

When Caroline turned eighteen, she was only a junior in high school. Now, as you know, that eighteenth birthday is a very big deal for most kids. As far as they're concerned, that's the day they leave childhood behind. Caroline was no exception. She felt that she should no longer have a curfew because, as she put it, "after all, I'm an adult now."

Our response was, "Caroline, I know you're upset about your curfew, but you're still in high school. We can certainly push the curfew back a little bit, but we're not going to get rid of it altogether." We finally agreed together that she could now stay out until 11:30 p.m. on weekends.

One night, not long after that, she came in at 11:45. She didn't call to tell us she was going to be late. She just walked in the door as if nothing was wrong. When we asked why she was late, she tried to shrug it off. "I'm not *that* late," she said. "It's only fifteen minutes."

"But, Caroline," we told her, "we agreed on 11:30. You came in at 11:45. That wasn't our agreement. So don't make any plans for next weekend because you'll be staying home!"

From that time until she graduated from high school and then married, Caroline was great about coming home at the agreed-upon time. She would always tell us what time she was coming in, and if that changed, she called and let us know. We are grateful that she became so considerate and happy that we confronted the issue of her curfew the first time it came up.

This situation illustrates one of two ways our children can learn what we expect of them: Simply tell them. Second, show them by example. Children feel more secure when they know what the rules are and what will happen when they break those rules.

Psychologist and author Dr. Paul Warren writes that "the toughest part of parenting teens is striking the right balance between permissiveness and rigidity." He goes on to say, "The right balance is usually characterized by reasonable boundaries about what is permitted and what isn't." We parents must communicate those boundaries to our kids.

4. As Much As Possible, Let Your Child Do Things for Herself

If you've ever attended a junior-high-school science fair, you know that either (a) today's seventh-graders are about one hundred times more talented than we were when we were kids, or (b) an awful lot of parents are doing their children's homework these days.

Undoubtedly there's some truth in that first statement. Today's students *are* smarter in science than we were. But it's clear that the second statement is also true.

One English teacher told us that he sees a tremendous difference between the papers his students write during class and the papers they write at home. And it's not just the fact that they have more time at home.

He reported that one mother who came in for a teacher-parent conference was angry that her son had received a C in his class. "She had a couple of papers he had written at home, papers for which he had received top marks. Then I showed her some of what he'd written in class. Most of it was incomprehensible, full of misspelled words, poor grammar, and incomplete thoughts. There wasn't much she could say after that."

I'm sure that mother was trying to do her son a favor by helping him with his homework. But what she was really doing was keeping him from learning how to write for himself. Rather than helping him, she was hindering his development. We're guilty of the same thing when we do things for our children that they ought to be doing for themselves or when we protect them from the consequences of their actions. As Jeannette Lofas writes in *Family Rules:*

> Stop rescuing kids from the consequences of their behavior. Some behaviors carry their own natural consequences; for example…missing the school bus, losing money, or forgetting work for school, all have consequences. The problem is that too many parents try to "fix it" for the child. They drive the child to a friend's house to retrieve the schoolbooks Adam left behind, or replace the money Marie lost, and so on. Don't do it.

Children must learn to be independent. That starts with simple things like taking care of their room. Author Ray Pelletier writes about a "Trust Bank" he established for his children. He says,

> The object was to teach them responsibility, and it worked this way: When they cleaned their room, came home from school on time, did their homework and chores and the other things they were supposed to do, what they were really doing was making deposits into the Trust Bank. On the other hand, if they hadn't done those things—for example, if yesterday one of them had come home from school an hour late—that was a major withdrawal from the Trust Bank. When Ray or Kim would come to me and tell me about something they really wanted to do—such as going to a friend's party—and if it seemed okay to me—I'd say, "Okay, I really want you to be able to do that, but let's see what's in the Trust Bank."

We've found that a plan like this works well when it comes to teaching responsibility. It also eliminates a lot of loud, angry parent-child discussions. Some children play the game of waiting for Mom and Dad to tell them to do something at least three times before they actually do it. But with a Trust Bank system, children have a clear understanding of what is expected of them before their parents even tell them, and they also know what the consequences will be if they fail to come through.

5. When Your Child Gets into Trouble, Don't Automatically Take His Side

A woman we know caught her daughter and another girl in a lie. Cindy and Loretta had told their mothers they were going to the movies. Instead they went off to a party they knew their parents would not allow them to attend.

When Cindy's mom found out what the girls had done, she felt obligated to call Loretta's mother and let her know about the situation. She was surprised when Loretta's mother responded coolly, "You must be mistaken about this."

When Cindy's mom said, "I just thought you might want to know about this," Loretta's mother responded angrily: "Maybe your daughter lies to you, but mine doesn't lie to me." Then she hung up, loudly.

Our friend figured she had done her duty. If the other mother didn't want to face up to her daughter's behavior, there wasn't anything more she could do about it. But she felt bad that Loretta's mom was refusing to face reality and wondered what the future held for her and her daughter. It's always a bit sad when you meet parents who think their children are perfect and who take their kids' side in any dispute. Someday a rude awakening is going to come for those parents!

We have already learned that whenever there is a conflict between one of our children and another person, it's important to listen carefully to both sides. When a child comes to us with a troubling situation involving an adult who has authority over them, we almost always side with the adult. We listen to the child. We ask questions. And we usually end with this one. "If we call Mrs. Guikema, what will she say happened?" Then we begin to get closer to the real story:

"Well, she'll probably tell you that I was acting silly in class."

"And were you?"

"I guess. Just a little."

"So you have to stay after school because you were misbehaving and not because your teacher was picking on you for no reason?"

"I was just trying to make the other guys laugh."

We parents can save ourselves a whole lot of embarrassment by talking to our kids to get to the bottom of a situation.

Similarly, when one of our children is involved in a conflict with another child, we first listen to what both kids have to say, and then we try to arbitrate a settlement. Most of the time we don't know whose story is closest to what really happened because we weren't on hand to witness the event that led to the problem. We do not automatically take one child's word over another's unless we have a very good reason to do that. We know that both children are usually exaggerating, but if we take the time to truly listen and ask a few questions, we can almost always get a good idea of where the truth lies.

One thing we do not allow our children to do is fight things out. We do not let them make loud accusations, use abusive or demeaning language, threaten each other in any way, or physically fight. They have to discuss the situation calmly. If they can't do that, then we simply tell them to stay out of each other's way until they can behave with more dignity.

Randall Hekman is a juvenile court judge who wishes parents would stop intervening for children who get into trouble with the law. He says, "Many of the kids who come into our courtroom will make recurring visits because their parents always 'cover' for them." He goes on to say that "the child who is so protected by parents…grows up with the feeling that he is immune to laws or rules. He can do as he wants because someone will be there to cover for him. That child will gradually lose his own self-esteem and will become less desirable to society."

Some parents subscribe to the conspiracy theory: If their child is in constant trouble, they assume it's because everyone is out to get her for some reason. But we realized a long time ago that this isn't likely. If one of our kids seems to be in trouble with everyone, it's probably because she deserves it.

We believe in standing by our kids and letting them know that we love them at all times, even when they've gotten themselves into trouble. If one of them has been treated unfairly or accused unjustly, he can count on our total, unflinching support. But, again, before we decide where we stand on a particular situation, we want to hear both sides of the story. We love our children dearly, but we also know that they're only human and that they do make mistakes.

6. BE UNDERSTANDING, BUT DON'T BE TOO QUICK TO MAKE OR ACCEPT EXCUSES

Have you ever noticed how some people tend to have one difficult experience after another, none of which are ever their fault?

Suppose you had a coworker who came in late three days in a row with a different excuse each day. On Monday his car wouldn't start. Tuesday he got stuck in traffic. On Wednesday his electricity went out during the night, and his alarm didn't go off. Wouldn't you start to think that the fellow just didn't try hard enough to get to work on time?

Well, if your children are giving you a steady stream of excuses about why they didn't do what you asked them to do, the same reasoning ought to apply. For example, not too long ago Gabi had a lot of excuses as to why she couldn't be ready to leave on time in the morning and why she couldn't seem to dress in her school uniform every day. We've had several calls from the school to come get her and bring her home so she can put on her uniform.

Caroline, who is older, used to drive the younger kids to school. She almost always had to honk the horn and nearly drag Gabi out of the house to get her to school before the first bell rang.

We finally got so tired of this daily routine that we had a conference with Gabi and told her that we would accept no more excuses. We explained that if she is not ready to leave with the rest of the kids at the proper time, she will have to walk to school. If that makes her late, she'll have to serve a detention. Furthermore, if she has to serve a detention for being late, she will be grounded from the phone for one week. Since we made the new rules, she has always been ready on time. It's amazing what a little motivation can do.

With nineteen children in the house, we understand that some excuses are valid. There are days when someone's car won't start. There are those occasions when traffic is jammed up. Occasionally something does go wrong, and the alarm doesn't go off when it's supposed to.

So we don't reject excuses out of hand. But if a child comes in after curfew two or three nights in a row, then he's going to be punished no matter what his excuses might be. If your child has a run of "bad luck" that keeps her from doing what she's supposed to do, it means that she's making poor decisions—and ultimately, she is the only one responsible for those decisions.

We simply refuse to let our children play the excuse game, blaming every-one and everything but themselves when they get into trouble. That game doesn't help anyone get where he wants to go in life, and we'd rather our children learned that from us now while the consequences are still relatively small.

When Caroline was in middle school, we got a call from one of her teachers who said she had been talking and laughing in class. When we confronted her, she said, "It's not my fault. The teacher seats me next to a boy who makes me laugh."

When Sarah was fifteen, she had the following excuse for not doing well in one of her classes: "It's not my fault the teacher doesn't know how to teach me right."

We had to laugh at both of those responses. Nice try, Caroline and Sarah, but neither one worked.

7. MAKE SURE YOUR CHILD KNOWS THAT HE'S NOT THE BOSS OF THE FAMILY

Every small child thinks the world revolves around her. But by the time she reaches school age, she ought to understand that this isn't the case. She should know that she's important, treasured, loved, and created in God's own image. But she should understand that she is not the center of the universe. She should know that the earth does not revolve around her, and neither does her family.

Although we have made plenty of mistakes along the way, nobody could ever accuse us of letting our children control the family. We try to take our children's feelings and desires into account, but we are the ones who make decisions that affect the whole family.

We've known parents who let their children control just about everything. They decide what's for dinner based on what the kids want. They let the children control the television. Vacations and weekend outings are planned according to their children's desires. It would be better for their children—and for their marriage—if these parents had done more of what they wanted to do and been less indulging of their children's whims.

8. Don't Back Down When She Puts You to the Test

A pastor who worked in a correctional facility for juvenile offenders asked some of the boys what parents could do to keep their children out of trouble. Among their answers: "Call our bluff," "Make it clear you mean what you say," "Don't compromise," "Don't be intimidated by our threats," "Stand up to us and we'll respect you," and "Kids don't want everything they ask for." Kids are often just testing the waters.

Have you ever had a conversation like the one that follows?

Teenage Daughter: Daddy, why won't you let me go to the party?

Father: Because there aren't going to be any parents there, and I don't want you at an unchaperoned party.

Teenage Daughter: Please, Dad! Everyone is going to be there.

Father: No, honey, I really don't think...

Teenage Daughter: Don't you trust me? I won't do anything wrong. I promise.

Father: I said...

Teenage Daughter: Please, Daddy! Please. It's means so much to me.

Father: Well, I guess maybe it won't hurt, just this once.

Almost everyone who's been a parent for any length of time can answer truthfully, "Been there, done that." But know that even though it's easier to give in, it's not good policy. Whenever we parents tell our children no about something and have a good reason for saying no, we should stick with it. That doesn't mean we don't have the right to change our minds. If we get new information that makes us rethink our original decision, we can be more than happy to change a no into a yes. But we realize that if one of our children knows he can always get us to give in to him, then he'll quickly reach the point where he disregards everything we say.

We are not doing our children (or ourselves) any favors when we cave in to them whenever the going gets tough. If one of our kids misbehaves and we tell him he's grounded for a week, then he *is* grounded for a week. There is no time off for good behavior even though having a grounded child around the house can be much harder on the parents than on the child.

Your children may not appreciate it now when you refuse to give in to them when they put you to the test. But they will appreciate it someday, and they will be much better off.

9. BE FIRM BUT NOT ABUSIVE WHEN HE'S PUSHED YOUR BUTTONS

Following this commandment is harder than it sounds. But you probably already know that. As Franklin P. Jones said, "You can learn many things from children: how much patience you have, for instance."

We try not to react in anger when our children have really done something to set us off. Most of the time we stop and take a deep breath. We can't say we've never screamed or yelled, but we try not to. And although we both believe in spanking when children are young, we avoided that whenever possible.

On my (Pat) way home from the office recently, I stopped by Albertson's to pick up some milk and a couple of other things we'd run out of. I was in line behind a guy who had left his children in the car. Obviously, like me, he was only planning to be in the store for a couple of minutes, and he had told his children not to get out of the car.

However, when we came out of the store, the kids had the car door open and his oldest boy was standing outside the car. The man absolutely blew his top. He began shouting at the top of his lungs for his son to "get back in that [expletive deleted] car."

He went on to shout, "You little [expletive deleted]. When we get home I'm going to [expletive deleted] whip your [expletives deleted]!"

Obviously frightened, the little boy jumped back in the car. "I'm sorry, Dad!"

But Dad kept on shouting, using the *F* word, the *S* word, the *GD* word, and yelling so loudly that people were coming out of the store to see what was going on.

I waited to see if the father was going to hit the child, because if he did I was going to intervene. I had just about made up my mind to go over and tell him he needed to calm down, but before I was able to do that, he got in the car, slammed the door, and peeled out, still yelling at the child in the backseat. By this time I was shaking with anger over what I had just witnessed.

Should this man have disciplined his son for disobeying? Certainly. But there is absolutely no way to justify treating a child that way, no matter what he has done. Stay cool. Stay calm. Count to ten if you have to. Be firm. But don't be nasty and foulmouthed.

10. Discipline Your Child Whenever She Breaks the Rules

This sounds like a no-brainer, and maybe it is. But for a while the prevailing child-rearing philosophy in this country was that there was no such thing as bad behavior. This philosophy was kind of like some Eastern religions which teach that there is really no such thing as evil, that evil is just a matter of perception. Disobedience, it was said, was related to intelligence. A child who broke all the rules was considered adventurous and bright. While it was okay to explain to him that his behavior had gone beyond what was acceptable, it was *not* okay to punish him. Doing so might discourage him, break his spirit, and deprive the world of a great genius. But when far too many of those "great geniuses" wound up either needing intensive psychotherapy or serving long stretches in prison, that philosophy of parenting was pretty much discarded.

Now most parents understand that, as Elisa Morgan and Carol Kuykendall said, "There are times when children simply need discipline." Morgan and Kuykendall go on to write, "Their actions ask for love, embedded in limits, and nothing else will do. For us parents, this means setting clear boundaries; then following through with logical consequences when our children overstep them. This process provides the 'training through containing' necessary for children to make good choices and to live life well."

As you've seen, some of our nineteen kids have been very frustrating to deal with over the years. We have many stories of struggle and pain. Parenting can look pretty bleak at times. But we've also had plenty of experiences of the kind of love that just melts your heart.

I (Pat) remember when our daughter Caroline came to us from Brazil on Christmas Day 1993. She was ten years old. She is a real sweetheart, a very tender and sensitive child. One summer afternoon, about six months after Caroline had come into our home, I was sitting with her and some of the other kids, watching a rented video of the movie *Annie,* the story of Little Orphan Annie's life in a Depression-era orphanage. When the movie ended, all the kids got up and ran out to go swimming—all except Caroline. She ran over, threw her arms around me, and sobbed her heart out.

"Hey, what's the matter?" I asked. "Why are you crying, honey?"

For a long time, she couldn't speak. Finally, she said, "I'm so glad I've got a daddy!"

That's when my eyes began to puddle up! That movie had brought back a lot of memories for her—recent memories of life on the streets and in the child welfare institutions of Brazil. Her horizon had been transformed from one of mere day-to-day existence to one of being loved, of belonging to a family, of having a daddy.

Chapter 10

PARENTS HAVE RIGHTS TOO!

Let there be space
in your togetherness.
KAHLIL GIBRAN

It's important to remember that parents have rights too. If we give and give and give some more to our children and never think of our own rights, it won't be long before we drop dead from exhaustion—or go broke! And neither one of those situations will do our children any good at all!

One mother, who rarely ever thought of herself, told us that her son had his own television, VCR, DVD, CD player, cell phone, and refrigerator in his room. She said that because his room is so nice, "When I punish him, I have to send him to *my room!*"

Another woman teased that her goal was "to give my kids everything I never had—and then move in with them."

If either one of the above comments reminds you of your life—if your kids have just about everything while you do without—then you need to start paying a bit more attention to meeting your own needs.

Think about it. Any time you travel by airplane, the flight attendants start things off by giving a little safety lecture. One of the things they tell you is that if something goes wrong with the air pressure in the cabin, an oxygen mask will drop from the ceiling. If you're traveling with a child, they say, put your own oxygen mask on first and then help your child with his mask. Why? Because it is only when your own needs are met that you can properly meet your child's needs.

Of course it is good to be willing to make sacrifices for your child, but that can be carried too far. Your children need you to be well rested, healthy, and in a positive frame of mind—and you can't be anything of those things if your personal needs are not being met. It's not selfish to take care of yourself. It is absolutely essential.

It is also absolutely essential that we teach our children to respect our rights. Although it's important to be accessible and available to our children, we cannot let them barge in and trample all over our rights any old time they feel like it. A good disciplinarian respects his children's rights, but he also lets them know that he expects the same respect from them in return.

Here are just a few of the rights all parents are entitled to.

You Have the Right to Privacy

You need some private space for the sake of your mental and spiritual health, but many parents make the mistake of letting their kids steal their privacy. They should not feel that it's all right to go through any of your belongings or use or borrow any of your things without asking you. In this high-tech day and age, when government officials and marketing firms seem to know almost everything there is to know about us, it's more important than ever to have some private space where you, and only you, can go.

Not too long ago our oldest, Stephanie, was home for the weekend. She watched as the younger kids kept coming to me (Ruth) for one thing or another. Finally, she said, "I hope you and Pat are going to have some time alone this weekend." I told her that we always make time to be alone. It's extremely important to keep the relationship focused and fresh.

You Have the Right to Be Respected

You deserve your child's respect simply because you are her parent. She wouldn't even be here if not for you! You also deserve respect because you are older, wiser, and stronger. You have the wisdom that comes from experience, and that alone is worthy of respect. (This, of course, doesn't apply to parents who are not worthy. There are some parents who, sad to say, don't deserve any respect at all.) Some parents think it's funny when their children sass them or even swear at them, but we don't. In order to become well-adjusted, successful adults, your children must have respect for those in authority—and that begins with you.

You Have the Right to Be Obeyed

It's fine if you want to explain to your children why you've established certain rules. You can, for example, let your son know that you don't want him riding his bike into the street because he might get hit by a car. Or you can explain to your teenage daughter that you need her to be home from her date by a certain time because you can't sleep until she gets home, and you have to get up to go to work in the morning. But you don't really have to explain anything. What it all comes down to in the end is that you're the parent, and the parent makes the rules. Period.

As we are writing this book, Caroline is now married. But when she was fourteen, she really put us to the test. (Have you noticed that most problems seem to occur when children are somewhere between thirteen and sixteen?)

I (Ruth) remember it this way: One morning after all the kids had left for school, I went around the house and straightened up their rooms. Caroline's bed wasn't made, which was unusual for her, so I decided to make it for her.

As I was doing that, I noticed something wrong with her blanket. It was much too small for her bed. How strange! We'd just bought it to go with her newly redecorated room, and it had fit perfectly when I'd made the bed for the first time. When I took the blanket off the bed for a closer look, I could see that someone had cut it in half.

As soon as Caroline got home from school, I asked her what had happened to her blanket. She answered, "I don't know what you mean. That's the way it was when we bought it."

I told her that I knew better—that someone had cut the blanket.

"Well, it wasn't me," she said.

I asked all of the other children if they had cut Caroline's blanket for some reason, but none of them knew anything about it.

"Caroline," I finally said in exasperation. "No one here knows anything about this blanket. Do you suppose someone broke into the house while we were gone, went straight to your room, and cut your blanket in two?"

"How should I know?" she shrugged. "All I know is that I didn't do it."

We couldn't figure it out. Why had Caroline cut the blanket—and why was she lying about it?

I told her I wanted her to think about what had happened and give me a plausible explanation within a couple of days. Until then she was grounded.

The next day, on the pretext that she needed something for school, Caroline asked our house manager, Angel, to drive her to Kmart, where we had bought the blanket in the first place. When she got home, she marched in and triumphantly handed me a note purportedly from the store manager. The note said something like, "This is the way the blanket looked when your daughter bought it."

I struggled to keep from laughing. First of all, the note was written on message paper from our house. Second, I could tell by the way it was worded that it hadn't been written by an adult. The signature was obviously fake. When Pat got home from work, I showed him the note, and we decided to confront the situation head on.

We took Caroline and the blanket to Kmart and asked to see the manager whose name was on the note. He was off, so we asked to see the manger of the linen department. When we showed her the blanket, she said, "Someone cut the blanket," which we already knew. (Duh!) At that point Caroline said the words we'd heard so many times over the past few days: "Well, I didn't do it!"

"But, Caroline," I said, "what about the note? Who wrote this? It's obviously not from the manager. He hasn't even been here today. And we know the blanket has been cut. What is going on?" Now she had two things to explain: the blanket and the note. But she just kept digging herself into a deeper hole.

When we finally got home, we told her she was grounded until she told us the truth. As it turned out, she was grounded for six months! Can you believe it? Six months!

Several times her brother Alan asked us, "What if Caroline doesn't tell you what happened by the time she's a senior in high school?"

"Then she'll be grounded until then."

"But that's three years!"

"That's all right. We're not going anywhere, and neither is she. We'll wait if we have to."

Finally, one day when Caroline and I were driving somewhere, she said, out of the blue, "I cut the blanket."

"What?"

"I cut the blanket."

"Why?" I asked. "And, more important, why have you been so stubborn about it?"

"I just didn't want you to know," she said. "I got carried away."

What happened was that she had met an eighteen-year-old boy who had asked her out on a date. We said no because we thought he was too old for her.

Nevertheless, she had spent quite a bit of time talking to him on the phone. She had even sneaked out one night to see him. He had given her one of his shirts to remember him by, and she had given him half of her blanket.

Caroline learned a few valuable lessons before this episode came to an end. One, don't sneak around. Two, don't lie. Three, don't forge other people's signatures. And four, no boyfriend is worth half your blanket. She gave up six months of her life for the sake of a lie. But since then she has been a complete jewel—honest, helpful, kind, and a joy to be around.

Every child hits a rough spot now and then. But if you hang in there, and refuse to give in, you can get them safely through the turbulent times.

YOU HAVE THE RIGHT TO TAKE TIME FOR EACH OTHER

We make sure that we have a date night every week and a date weekend every other month. This time together is absolutely necessary to keep our marriage in tiptop shape. Admittedly, there are days when all we want is to go back to bed—when it's been one thing after another from the time the alarm clock buzzed us awake in the morning.

It's not always easy to give each other the attention we need when we're running in different directions and trying to keep things from spinning completely out of control. That's why husbands and wives need time for romance, time to just be silly together, time to laugh, and time to get away from the daily pressures that come from being a parent.

If you are not presently seeing to it that you and your spouse have some time on a regular basis for just the two of you, take our advice and start planning those little getaways right now—at least one a week. They are essential.

It's also good for children to see you "dating" and showing love. They need to see just how much you love each other. If they see you embrace or share a kiss, they may say something about being embarrassed—but deep down they love it.

Shortly after Pat and I were married, Stephen left me a note that says it all:

> Thank you for being so good to Dad and us. Life has been such a joy since you've been here. It makes me really happy when I see you and Dad kissing and enjoying each other. It's been a long time since Dad has been truly happy. I can't thank you enough, and I thank God that He brought you into our lives.

If children are to build their own successful relationships in the future, they need to see one in action now. Role models are important, so be a romantic role model for your kids. They have a right to it.

YOU HAVE THE RIGHT TO DISCIPLINE YOUR CHILDREN

Some parents don't impose discipline on their children because they are afraid their kids will hate them. But as the late actress Bette Davis wrote, "If you have never been hated by your children, you have never been a parent."

In the book *Teens Can Bounce Back,* speaker/author Josh McDowell writes, "The child whose father provides godly discipline—discipline that is loving, clear, consistent—is likely to reap a harvest of respect, peace, and righteousness. He equips his children to learn self-discipline, a quality that will help them lead lives that are healthy—emotionally, socially, spiritually, and physically. He helps his children avoid the often-tragic consequences of unwise behavior. He enables his children to enjoy the blessing of a good reputation. He promotes harmony in his children's minds and hearts and in their relationships with others."

We've already mentioned that our son Alan is one who has always pushed hard against the limits. On one particularly difficult occasion, we wrote him this letter:

Alan,

We love you very much and want you to have a good life. However, we know that if you keep doing what you've been doing, you will have a hard life. We have tried talking to you, but you say that doesn't do any good. And you've also said you don't really care. You are mad because you feel your punishment is too severe. We don't think you realize just how bad your behavior has been, so we decided to put it in writing. Here are the reasons you've been grounded.

1. The fight at school.
2. Using the *F* word.
3. Singing a nasty song.
4. Being rude and disrespectful to your teacher.
5. Cheating on your schoolwork.

So you see, Alan, there are five things you've done. Because of the fight, you were grounded for two weeks—no phone, no friends, no television. Starting fights is serious. It could put you in jail, so the grounding was serious. After that you used the *F* word, so we added another week. After we met with your teacher, we removed the Play-Station 2 and the stereo. You only lost two more things, but you did three things: singing the song, being rude, and cheating.

What you must understand is that we will no longer stand for any of this kind of behavior. If you have not turned your behavior around by June 11, we will send you to boot camp—it's from 7 a.m. to 7 p.m. every Saturday—until your behavior changes.

You can do this. You know how to act. This year has been a really good year until this past month. Please understand that if you continue with this kind of behavior, you will not get your privileges back and you will go to boot camp. Please let us know that you understand this very clearly. Ask questions and get it all cleared up so you know what you need to do.

> We love you,
> Mom & Dad

We did our best to explain that we were not picking on him. He was being disciplined—fairly—for behaviors that we could not and would not tolerate. Here is his response:

> Mom & Dad,
> I am sorry for all the troubles I have caused. It will never happen again. I understand why you are mad at me. Please forgive me. I know that you are trying to help me understand what life is all about. Thank you for being hard on me.
> Alan

We wish we could report that things have been perfect since this exchange of letters. But we are all still working on it. Alan understands that when he steps out of line, he will be disciplined. He also understands that we discipline him because we love him and want him to be the best person he can possibly be. As for us, we understand that Alan is struggling to improve his behavior and that he really does know where we are coming from.

For discipline to be effective, it must be administered with love. It has been said that rearing a child is like rowing a boat. One oar is marked *disci-*

pline; the other is marked *love.* In order to get the boat headed in the right direction, you have to use both oars. If you only use one of them, the boat will just go around in circles and you won't get anywhere.

Bill Bright, who, along with his wife, Vonette, founded Campus Crusade for Christ, was a longtime family friend until his death in 2003. One time, when Bill and Pat were talking about the joys and trials of parenting, Pat mentioned that it took plenty of discipline to raise nineteen kids.

He remembers that Dr. Bright "simply looked at me in that quiet way of his and said, 'Don't forget the love.' "

PRACTICE THE "BEST METHOD" OF COMMUNICATION

We've mentioned before that we strive to be constructive, rather than destructive, in all of our dealings with our children. If we must discipline, we want to do it in love. When criticism is necessary, we want it to be offered in a helpful, rather than hurtful, way. We also want our children to be constructive and positive in their relationships with one another.

And that's what the BEST Method is all about. These guidelines for interpersonal relationships were developed by Dr. Ed Wheat in his excellent book *Love Life for Every Married Couple.* He says that this method is a way of setting the family "thermostat" at a proper temperature, so that everyone is comfortable. The BEST Method consists of:

- Blessing
- Edifying
- Sharing
- Touching

Blessing
There are four specific ways to bless your family. They are:
1. Speak well about every member of your family and respond to them with positive words in every situation.
2. Go out of your way to do kind things for one another.

3. Tell the members of your family why you appreciate them and that you are thankful for them.

4. Pray for God's highest blessing in every family member's life.

Pat's friend Bill Glass, the evangelist and former NFL star, has strong feelings about blessing your children. He suggests using the following four phrases regularly. He says that if children don't hear these things, they will have an emptiness in their souls. Here are the four statements:

1. "You belong to me, and I'm glad."

2. "You're a winner, and I'm proud of you."

3. "You have value, and I delight in you."

4. "I love you, and I think you're terrific."

Think about what might happen if a child heard these words on a regular basis while growing up. It would be much easier for her to fight off the villains of the world. It would be much easier to ignore temptation. It would be much easier not to be hurt by harsh words from others. Life would be easier just knowing that someone felt this way about you.

Television personality Katie Couric said, "I grew up knowing I was someone special. All the kids in our family did." By letting her know she was special, her parents paved the way for her to excel in life.

Try these four statements on your kids. See what happens.

Edifying

This means, simply, to support or build up.

We talked earlier about the importance of being a cheerleader for your kids. It's also important to be a cheerleader for your spouse. Dad, does your wife know that you think she's beautiful? Does she know that you think she's a terrific cook? Or that you appreciate her heart for God? Mom, does your husband know that you appreciate him for how hard he works? Does he know that you'd marry him all over again? Do you let him know that you appreciate the work he does around the house?

Don't let your appreciation go unexpressed. Don't tell yourself that your

Chapter 11

THE PRODIGAL SON...
OR DAUGHTER

Now I know I've got a heart because it's breaking.
THE TIN MAN

A second-grade teacher asked her students what they wanted to be when they grew up.

Immediately an excited chorus of responses came from kids all over the classroom: "A doctor!" "An astronaut!" "A fireman!" "I want to be the president." And so on.

It seemed that all the students—except little Tommy—knew exactly what they wanted to be. He sat silently at his desk.

"Tommy," the teacher asked. "How about you? What do you want to be when you're grown up?"

"Possible," Tommy answered quietly.

"Possible?" the teacher asked, uncertain that she had heard him correctly.

"Yes," Tommy explained. "My mom is always telling me that I'm impossible...so when I grow up, I want to be possible."

It's a cute story—and one that many parents and children can identify with. All parents want their children to be happy. We want to be proud of their accomplishments and help them feel "possible"—as if anything they want to do in life is within reach.

And for the most part, children want their parents to be proud of them. They are happiest when their behavior pleases their parents.

Sadly, there are exceptions, and that's what this chapter is all about. Some children choose to be "impossible." When they do, it's important to remember—we'll say it again—that this is your child's choice, not yours. You do not have to blame yourself for everything your child does. If your child gets in trouble, it does not mean you are a bad parent.

It hurts terribly when a child becomes openly rebellious, and it makes you wonder, "How in the world did it ever come to this?" Your adventure in parenthood certainly didn't start out this way.

When you first gaze upon your beautiful newborn daughter through the nursery window, your heart seems to melt within you. Or when the orphanage finally puts that small hand into yours and says you can take that cute little boy home with you, you feel that you're going to burst with joy. Just looking at this new life, so helpless and so dependent upon you, makes you grateful beyond words. God is so good! What a gift he has bestowed!

On the day your daughter is born, it is impossible to imagine that one day she will look at you with rage in her eyes, stomp her feet, and shout, "I hate you!"

But she might.

Or think about the day you will watch your first-grader bravely climb aboard his school bus for the first time. When he reaches the top step and turns around, you see the fear and uncertainty in his eyes—and there are tears in your own. For a moment, you want him to get off the bus, run into your arms, and be your baby for just a few more days.

As you stand there with a lump in your throat, watching the bus roll away, you could never imagine that a few years from now, he will be testing every single one of your rules to the breaking point—and beyond. How could that precious little angel grow up to be the boy who complains that you're always on his back and asks you to please drop him off two blocks from school in the morning, because he doesn't want to be seen with you?

Such is parenting.

EVERY PARENT FACES CHALLENGES

If the picture we've just painted makes you feel discouraged, keep in mind that your experience of parenting may not be quite as bad as this. But be assured that every parent runs into some rough spots sooner or later. And the truth is that as children enter the "rebellious years," most parents begin to sympathize with the mother eagle and understand why she eventually kicks the fledglings out of the nest.

There are certain days when, if you asked us what it was like to raise teenagers, we'd tell you to multiply the terrible twos by eight and add a driver's license. The preacher asked his congregation, "Why did Abraham take Isaac to be sacrificed when the boy was twelve years old?" The answer: "Because if Isaac were a teenager, it wouldn't have been a sacrifice."

Now, parenting teens back in the eighties, when the oldest of our clan were teenagers, was a piece of cake, a walk in the park, a day at the beach, compared to parenting teens now. There's only one way to get your kids through the minefield of life here in the opening years of the twenty-first century, and that is to love them so much that you're willing to be tough with them when you need to be.

Our friend Fran Silvernell, former director of property management for the RDV Sportsplex—where the Orlando Magic have their offices—is a father who knows the pain of dealing with a prodigal child. Fran's daughter Candi was a superathlete in several sports, a girl who had college scouts coming to her games during her sophomore year in high school. Fran remembers, "She was so excited about the future, and so was I." Candi was also a good student and a beautiful young woman. The future seemed limitless.

Then, when she was sixteen, she met a boy, and according to Fran, "ran away from home and from sports." Thus began seven years of heartache.

Fran says, "Candi is now twenty-three years old. She has been on her own since she was sixteen. She's been in trouble with the law a couple of times, mostly for fighting with boyfriends. She has told me many times she wishes she had a life rewind button."

Fran candidly admits, "I would not be honest if I were to say that I'm not disappointed in the way her life has turned out. On the other hand, she is a good person, loves her family, and wishes she didn't have to struggle so hard right now. My heart is heavy, but she will figure it out… It's up to her."

Our Orlando broadcaster friend John Adams is the last guy you'd ever expect to lose it with anybody. He's a loving, Christian father of four. Yet he tells, with obvious regret, about the time one of his daughters threatened to run away from home so she could be with a boy he felt was of questionable moral character.

John says, "When I went to her room to check on her, I found her packing a bag. Again I told her she would not be allowed to leave, and I blocked her way. She started opening the window to escape. I intervened and eventually she was literally in my face, and while the two of us were arguing, she told me to shut up. Acting on impulse I slapped her on her left cheek. She told me she was going to call the police and report me for child abuse. I invited her to go ahead and call 911, which she did, and three cars and four police officers came to the house. They concluded they were dealing with a rebellious teenager and that it might be better if she were allowed to leave for the evening. I agreed, knowing she would try to slip out the window if I refused."

Thus began several weeks in which the girl stayed with friends until she had "worn out her welcome," and then she returned home. "She is home, but she knows where we stand," John says. "We've let her know that we love her very much, but we cannot tolerate such behavior in our house."

He knows that the battle is probably not over, and although he regrets very much having slapped his daughter, any parent of a prodigal child knows how quickly you can get pushed to the edge of the precipice.

OUR STORY

One of our sons is a prime example of a prodigal child. He began having problems in about the fifth or sixth grade. He is one of the brightest people you could ever meet, yet he's been in almost every kind trouble: sneaking out, taking illegal drugs, lying, stealing, cutting classes, refusing to do his homework—and more. We tried moving him to different schools. We even sent him away to military school until his senior year in high school so he wouldn't have a negative impact on his younger brothers and sisters. We took him to counseling. We spent hours praying that he would change his behavior. No matter what we did, he always chose to get right back into trouble.

Before he began his senior year of high school, he begged us to come home. He had been away at military school for several years, and he wanted his last year before college to be spent with the rest of the family. We talked about this for quite a while, with each other and with him. We wanted him to come home, but we were afraid of what would happen if he did. If we let him come home and he began behaving as he had before, we wouldn't be able to send him back to the military school. We might destroy all the progress he'd made. Even so, we finally agreed that he could come home if he would honestly try to live by our rules. We even put in writing what we expected of him and asked him to sign a contract with us. No problem. He was happy to sign.

Looking back on it now, we suppose we should have known better. Signing that paper didn't really mean a thing to him. But it is hard not to err on the side of compassion when your children are involved. A few weeks after he returned home, we discovered that he had been sneaking out—again—from a small window in his room that opened out to the roof. We tried to stop the behavior by having our house manager nail the window shut.

Our son responded by pulling out the nails.

When we confronted him about his behavior, he said he needed more freedom; he was old enough to be out at night with his friends if that was where he wanted to be. We told him that wasn't the way things worked at our house. If he was going to live under our roof, he had to abide by our rules.

We had the window removed and replaced it with a solid wall—only to have him start sneaking out of a tiny bathroom window and climbing down from the roof. It was not only disobedient. It was dangerous, too.

Well, we had a cabinet built over that window.

Unfortunately we couldn't cover all the windows in the house, and he always found some way to escape. He denied that he was going out at night, but that was pretty easy to disprove since he often left footprints on the inside of the windowsill.

Another discussion about his "need for freedom" versus our house rules ensued. We told him that freedom came with trust and that we simply couldn't trust him because, when we did, he always let us down. He asked if we could wipe the slate clean and start over. He'd show us what he could do. We agreed to start somewhere in the middle. We would give him a few privileges, see how he handled them, and then move on to bigger and better things. We did this, remembering the words of Christ, who said, "Whoever can be trusted with very little can also be trusted with much, and whoever is dishonest with very little will also be dishonest with much" (Luke 16:10). For a time it seemed as if this new arrangement was working.

We were so relieved when we finally got him to the night of his highschool graduation. Sadly, we had no idea what had been going on behind the scenes. We had caught him breaking a number of our rules, but he was doing much more that we didn't catch. He was so smart and so conniving that he could look us straight in the eye and tell a whopper of a lie without even flinching.

On graduation night he told us he wanted to go camping with some friends and promised that he'd be careful. We warned him about all the accidents and arrests that take place on graduation night. We told him that graduation is one of the most dangerous nights of the year for high-school seniors, even more dangerous than prom night and homecoming.

He said he understood and headed out for an evening of "safe fun" with his friends.

At 3:00 a.m. the phone rang.

The dispassionate voice on the other end informed us that our son had been arrested for possession of marijuana. We fought the impulse to run right down and bail him out of jail. We figured he needed a little time to think about what he'd done, so we didn't bring him home until noon the next day.

For the next ninety days, his actions were restricted by the court. He was confined to our house, leaving only to attend some summer classes at a local community college and go to his job. His driver's license was taken away, so we had to drive him everywhere he went. He was ordered to attend Narcotics Anonymous and see a counselor.

We hoped and prayed that this would finally be the turning point of his life. Surely he would see that he couldn't continue down the path he had chosen. But instead he argued that marijuana was completely harmless and that there was no reason it should be illegal. He felt that his arrest was stupid.

Still, we were shocked when, two weeks after his arrest, he was asked to undergo a drug test and failed. He said the test was wrong and swore that he hadn't been using drugs, but his probation officer warned him that if he tested positive again, he would go back to jail. He was randomly drug tested several times during the next ninety days and never tested positive again. Naturally this made us hopeful—again—that he wasn't really dependent on drugs and that he'd discovered he could live without them.

He had been planning on enrolling in a state university in the fall, but he wasn't able to do that because he was still under house arrest. So he continued taking classes at the local community college. He made two A's during the summer and was making A's and B's during September and October. We started talking about buying him a car when he left for the state university at the end of the semester. After all, we could see that he was making tremendous progress.

Or so we thought.

Sadly, after his probationary period ended in October, his life again began to slide downhill. By the end of November he was failing two classes and not coming home when he was supposed to. We suspected he was back to using marijuana, which he denied. He said he was still planning to go to the state university in January.

We told him we couldn't pay for school if he wasn't going to take it seriously. Nor could we give him a car until his behavior improved. We told him that we'd be happy to continue paying for his classes at the community college. Once he proved he could settle in and do the work there, we'd be happy to pay the higher costs associated with a university education.

Instead of accepting our offer, immediately after Christmas he dropped out of school and moved out of our house. He lived off one of his brothers for almost five months before he finally got a part-time job. We're not sure how much money he made, but we know it wasn't much. And we're pretty sure that however much it was, most of it went to support his bad habits. We have called several times to check on him, but he never has much to say, and he doesn't call us unless he needs something.

One time he called and asked if he could borrow money for a rent deposit. He said he'd pay it back within a couple of weeks. As of this writing, that was about six months ago, and we haven't seen a penny. Nor do we expect to. We gave him the money as a test, just to see how he would handle it. Unfortunately he handled it the way we thought he would—the wrong way.

Some people might wonder how we could let our son move out and drop out of school. Our answer is that he's almost twenty. We have found that once a child reaches that age, his parents can't really make him do anything. He can either choose to follow his parents' guidelines, because he wants to and because he respects his mom and dad, or he can choose to disregard those guidelines.

We were about to write on this page that nothing has changed with our son and that we simply have to persevere in hope and prayer, but just as this book was going to press, we had a major breakthrough with him. After over a year of no contact, I (Pat) nervously called our son to invite him to have dinner with me. Surprisingly, he accepted, and our dinner went very well. We talked for two hours, and our conversation was friendly and cordial and warm. I was ecstatic.

So, the bottom line is that much of parenting is just hanging in there and not panicking, letting the kids grow and expand. There really can be happy reunions like this one!

The "Oppositional" Child

Such a son or daughter has been labeled "an oppositional child" by Dr. William Carter in his book *Child Think*. An oppositional child is in constant conflict with adults and refuses to cooperate with her parents. Just about the only consistency she ever shows is disobedience. This child doesn't care about what is right or wrong. All that matters to her is the way her behavior makes her feel. It doesn't matter what her parents say or what society thinks. The oppositional child does not respond to normal discipline. She refuses to give up her stubborn, disobedient behavior even when it would be to her advantage to do so.

Another characteristic of oppositional children is that they blame everyone else for their poor decisions. This is exactly what our son does. Although we love him very much, he doesn't believe that's true, and he even blames us for his current situation. He doesn't see that we want him to have a good life or that he's the one choosing not to.

Our son has been raised according to our principles and guidelines. He's been loved and nurtured. He's been praised. We've talked to him for hours to try to keep the lines of communication open. He's been punished. He's been asked to sign contracts with us. He's been through counseling. We've done everything we can to love him out of his behavior, but nothing has worked. That's when tough love has to kick in. If you don't use tough love, you become an enabler. You get in the way of cause-and-effect lessons that could be learned. It is vital that children reap the consequences of their actions.

There is only one solution to the prodigal's behavior, and that is to withdraw all the support that makes his destructive behavior possible. That's what we have tried to do, even though it hurts terribly to step back and do nothing while our child is struggling.

Tough love requires refusing to help your wayward child continue in her wrong behavior and refusing to allow yourself to be victimized. It may even mean cutting off contact with your child until she changes her behavior, even though that can be nerve-racking. (Unfortunately some of our prodigal children had other enablers in their lives. When that happens, the recovery period will be much longer and much harder—if it ever happens at all.)

During these times of little or no communication with our children, we have clung to Jesus' story of the prodigal son in Luke 15:11-32. In this parable, it wasn't until the repentant son turned from his lifestyle and returned home that the father showered him with love and welcomed him back with open arms. While the son was still living in rebellion in a distant country, that father did not send money to him so he could continue to live it up. He allowed his son to sink into the mud of the pigpen so the boy could find out what the real world is all about.

In his book *Loving a Prodigal,* H. Norman Wright tells the story of a teenager named Connie who ran away to Canada with a girlfriend one summer because she felt her parents were smothering her. When winter came, bringing with it snow, wind, and plummeting temperatures, Connie called her parents and told them she wanted to come home.

Her parents reacted without anger (by the way, rebellious kids love anger) and said they would be delighted to see her again, but they did not offer to send her an airline ticket home.

"How will I get home?" Connie asked.

"Well, honey," her mom replied, "how did you get there?"

"I thumbed it," Connie replied, obviously expecting her mom to gasp in horror and rush to rescue her so she didn't have to travel that way again.

Instead her mother replied, "Well, Connie, how do you plan to get home?"

"I don't know," the girl replied, a tremor in her voice.

"Is there something we can do?"

"I'd like you to help."

"Hmmm," her mother answered. "I've always felt that if you got yourself somewhere, you should be able to get yourself back. However, I would be willing to send you half the fare for a bus trip home if you found out how much it would cost. Of course we'll send it directly to the bus company."

There was silence on the other end of the line. But Mom wasn't done. "And of course you'd have to pay us back with interest after you returned home and got a job here."

After another moment of silence, Connie said, "Okay. I'll find a job, and I'll get home on a bus." Then she made a point to tell her parents that her friend had already gone home, courtesy of an airline ticket from her parents.

"I know, dear," Mom said. "But this is what we're willing to do. You got yourself there by thumbing. The bus trip would probably be better than that, right?"

Connie sighed, "I guess you're right."

That was tough love. Of course Connie's parents wanted their daughter home as quickly as possible. But that wouldn't have taught her anything. Instead they would have enabled her and probably set her up to run away again the next time she encountered problems at home.

Without realizing it, we did a lot of rescuing and enabling of our son in the beginning because we thought we were showing love. We've discovered since then that although tough love is a very difficult path to walk, it is the only path that helps the prodigal find his way back home.

CHARACTERISTICS OF A PRODIGAL

In his book, Dr. H. Norman Wright offers descriptions of wayward sons and daughters based on passages from the book of Proverbs. If you're wondering whether your son or daughter fits the description of a prodigal (the Bible uses the word *fool*), check these out:

1. A fool hates learning; he already knows it all and doesn't need to learn anything else (see Proverbs 1:22).

2. A fool is defensive all the time; when corrected, she rejects what is said (see Proverbs 16:22).

3. A fool thinks he knows everything and therefore doesn't listen to anyone. He laughs at the system; he opposes the law and the legal system (see Proverbs 12:15; 15:5).

4. A fool doesn't learn because she is so distracted by her lifestyle (see Proverbs 17:24).

5. A fool can't control his tongue and gets angry easily (see Proverbs 29:11; 12:16; 20:3; 22:24-25; 10:14).

6. A fool has no self-control. She's impulsive and has no regard for anyone else's feelings (see Proverbs 27:3).

7. A fool makes senseless, ridiculous comments; there is no depth (see Proverbs 1:28; 18:7).

8. A fool is full of pride; he's full of himself (see Proverbs 14:3).

9. A fool cannot handle success; she will sabotage herself every time because success is right. She wants to be wrong. She likes breaking the rules (see Proverbs 26:1).

10. A fool cannot handle money, so don't give him any (see Proverbs 19:10). (We've certainly learned this lesson.)

If these comments describe your child, you're probably wondering if the prodigal can ever change. The answer is yes, but *you* can't change him. Only your child—with God's help—can do that. And sometimes God allows our wayward boys and girls to go through some really tough times in order to bring them around to a correct way of thinking about life.

Our daughter Sarah is a good example of this. When she was sixteen, Sarah began dating a boy who was not good for her. We told her he would get her into trouble, but she wouldn't listen. We tried to keep her away from him, but she began sneaking out. Then one night she didn't come home at all, so we called the police and reported her missing. As we were filling out the paperwork, she walked into the house as if nothing had happened. The police officer talked with her about curfews and the importance of obeying her parents, but she did not respond in a good way and instead was angry that we had reported her missing.

The next several months consisted of one battle after another until Sarah finally moved out to live with her boyfriend and his mother. We let her take her clothes, but nothing else. We didn't give her any money, but we told her that she was welcome to come home anytime she was willing to follow our rules. We were dying inside as we watched her go, but the constant fighting was consuming energy and attention required by our fifteen other children still living at home.

Almost as soon as she moved out, she quit going to school and got a job as a waitress to support herself. We heard rumors that her boyfriend was in a gang and that Sarah was actually in the middle of a fight where gunfire was exchanged. We were sick at heart and prayed daily for her safety and her return home. We heard that the boyfriend was in jail, but still Sarah continued to live with his mother.

One day she came home to talk, and we were thrilled, hoping that her appearance meant a change of attitude. But all she really wanted was for us to use our influence to get her boyfriend out of jail. When we said no, she stormed off saying that we never did anything for her.

Over the next few years, we had very little contact with Sarah. We got news about her from some of our other kids, but she wouldn't come to see us—not even on Thanksgiving or Christmas.

Finally one day she came by to say hello, and we could tell right away that there was something different about her. She wasn't the smiling, happy girl we used to know, but she was pleasant. She had continued to work in the restaurant business and was doing okay. We started going to the restaurant where she was working to see her occasionally, and that year she came home for Christmas with a new (improved) boyfriend.

Last year, as we were sitting at her restaurant, she came up to Pat and said, "Daddy, guess what? I got my GED!" We were thrilled and said yes when, sometime later, she asked if we would help her take classes at the community college. She even moved into our guesthouse to live, and she sometimes helps with the younger children.

As we write this, she's working in the restaurant, taking college classes, and apparently getting her life in order. She now tells her younger brothers and sisters to listen to us and do what we say because "life is hard out there."

What we've learned from all this is that when a child becomes a prodigal of his own free will, he has to return of his own free will. It is the child's choice. All we can do is show tough love and pray that God will open the child's mind so he can finally see the truth. Then, and only then, can we welcome him home with open arms and enjoy a right relationship with him.

We have shared the story of two of our prodigals, one on the way to recovery and one in the holding pen. We have been down this road several other times. In every instance we practice tough love. We refuse to fund a lifestyle that we believe is wrong. We will not pay for insurance, car payments, rent, or anything else until there is evidence of real change—although we gladly do all of these things and more for our children who choose to live the right way. As Oprah Winfrey said in the May 2003 issue of her magazine, "The great challenge [of parenting] isn't just having a child. It's giving that child exactly what he or she needs to grow into a confident, self-loving adult who can offer something back to the world."

Most of our children are giving something back to the world. They are productive, contributing human beings who make us feel both grateful and proud. As for our prodigals, we pray earnestly for their complete recovery and their return to the wonderful way of life that honors God.

PART FIVE

The Blessings
of Responsible Behavior

Chapter 12

"What, Me? Responsible?"

Building Character and Other

Parenting Challenges

A time comes when you need to stop waiting for the man you want to
become and start being the man you want to be.

BRUCE SPRINGSTEEN

When Caroline was in the tenth grade, she had a difficult time in her biology class. Her other grades were good, but science was definitely not her strong point. We could both sympathize because neither one of us is especially gifted in science either.

Caroline was growing more discouraged with every day that passed. Then one night at dinner, she announced, "Mr. Rogers [her biology teacher] is really messing up my GPA!"

Does that sound familiar?

One thing we have seen again and again in dealing with our children—and especially with our teenagers—is that they don't want to take responsibility for anything unless they see clearly that it's in their best interest to do so. They will argue, deny, shift blame, and insist, "It wasn't my fault," when they really need to say, "I'm sorry. I messed up. Please forgive me."

As parents we are continually frustrated, baffled, and at times angered by the seeming illogic behind this universal teenage trait. But once we parents accept irresponsibility as a fact of life for most teenagers and stop trying to argue with them on their terms, we are in a position to begin teaching them how to become responsible adults. It's not easy—but it can be done.

As a consultant for the FranklinCovey Company, I (Ruth) teach *The Seven Habits of Highly Effective People* in corporate settings all over the country. Habit #1 is Be Proactive. We are practicing this habit when we take responsibility for our own lives. People who are proactive don't blame everyone else for the way their life is turning out. They don't try to slide through life clutching someone else's coattails. We teach our children that because they are responsible for their own success, they need to take control of their lives.

As Dr. Seuss says, "You have brains in your head. You have feet in your shoes. You can steer yourself toward any direction you choose."

Is it hard to take control of your own life? Yes.

Will you fall down along the way? Absolutely.

Will you sometimes want to give up? Without a doubt.

But will it be worth it? Definitely.

Why is it that one child grows up to be just an ordinary, middle-of-the-pack type of adult while another becomes an outstanding leader like Theodore Roosevelt or Mother Teresa? The answer to that question often comes down to one word: responsibility. Some people develop a responsible attitude very early in life. Others never become responsible at all.

The story is told about a man who fathered two little boys before he was convicted of a serious crime and sent off to prison, where he spent most of the rest of his life. For many years neither one of those little boys had any contact with their father. The first boy graduated from college, developed a successful career, and became known as a devoted family man. The second boy followed his father's footsteps into a career as a criminal and, like his dad, wound up in prison.

That's when a newspaper reporter checked into the background of both boys, trying to determine what had caused them to take such divergent paths in life. When the reporter asked the first young man why he had done so well in life, he replied, "What else could I have become, with a father like mine?"

When the same question was put to the second son, he replied, "What else could I have become, with a father like mine?"

These boys had the same genetic makeup. They were reared by the same mother in the same environment. Yet their lives turned out so differently. Why? Because one became positively proactive in life and chose a path of responsibility, while the other abdicated responsibility and chose to blame others for his own failures. We can do all we can to influence our children, but in the end, the path they take in life is a choice they must make.

GROWING UP

One goal for us as parents is to get our children to become positive and proactive. But how do we know if they're getting it? You know your child is growing up when:

- You no longer have to pry him out of bed to get ready for school in the morning, and he seems to understand that a good education and a good future go hand in hand.
- You don't have to remind her thirty-seven times every night to get her homework done.
- He goes out on his own to look for an after-school or summer job because he doesn't want to depend on you for his spending money.
- She tells you that she appreciates everything you do for her even when she doesn't want something from you.
- She borrows the car and brings it back with a full tank of gas because "the needle was almost to E."
- He mows the lawn without being asked because he noticed the grass was getting long.
- You come home from work to find that she's vacuumed the house and washed a load of laundry just because she wanted to help out.
- He insists on taking you out to dinner because you do so much for him—and then he actually pays for it!

These are just some of the amazing events that happen sooner or later along every parent's journey through life. (Absolute truthfulness leads us to admit that it's usually later.) Such are the wonderful moments that let you know you've done a pretty good job as a parent after all and that your children are well along the road to responsible adulthood.

Mark Twain once said that when he was a boy, he thought his father was one of the most ignorant men on earth. But when he reached his midtwenties he was amazed at how much the man had learned in ten years.

Similarly, as our children begin to grow into responsible adults, they usually see for the first time that we really do know a thing or two about life. It is gratifying when they begin to understand how hard we have worked to provide and care for them and to recognize the struggles we have endured on their behalf.

When Caroline got her driver's license, I (Ruth) was delighted by her willingness to take over some of the carpool duties. Like most teenagers she loved to drive, so she offered to take her younger brothers and sisters to some of their games and other activities.

Unfortunately her joy over having the job of transportation captain was short-lived. One day, only two months after getting her driver's license, Caroline came home in a horrible mood. When I asked what was wrong, she frowned and sighed, "Mom, do you know what it's like driving around with three whining kids?"

I had to laugh. "Why, yes, dear. I have done that on occasion."

She didn't say anything in response, but I saw the light of understanding come into her eyes. She realized that our life wasn't always a day at the beach. She was getting her first taste of what it's like to be an adult and a parent, and I could see that her appreciation of us had grown as a result.

Yes, your children will grow into responsible adults. But how do you help them get there? And how do you cope until they do? The number one thing you can do—and the number one thing we strive for—is simply this: Set a good example for your kids.

Dr. Jay Kessler has this good advice for us: "A lot of parents ask me: 'What can I do to get my kids to be more like me?' I tell them, 'Your kids will be like you, so the real question is, 'How can I be the kind of parent I should be, so that my kids will be the right kind of people when they are imitating me?' "

REMEMBER THAT SOMEONE'S WATCHING

Just before Mother's Day a few years ago, a major greeting card company went to a men's prison and offered the inmates free cards and postage to send those cards to their mothers. So many men came for cards that the entire supply was handed out in a few minutes. The event was so successful that the card company decided to try it again, this time on Father's Day.

This time nobody came. Not one prisoner wanted to send a card to his dad!

Bill Glass, who has devoted years of his life to prison ministry, said he's never met an inmate who loved his father. In fact, they all hate their fathers. Can you imagine that! What an important and sad lesson about what happens when fathers abdicate their responsibility toward their sons, when fathers don't set the loving example that God requires of them. Now we're not telling this story to pick on men or to say that dads don't love their kids as much as moms do. Rather, we're telling it because it is a startling example of just how important a father can be in the life of his children. *Father* means "the one who gives me strength." Every child needs to draw strength from a father who is a good mentor and role model.

As Washington Redskins coach Joe Gibbs said, "Intentionally or not, children tend to emulate their parents. Whether you foster good relationships or poor ones in your home, your children will sit up and take notice. They will see and remember the way you treat your wife or husband; the way you speak to and about your family members; and the way you express love, joy, pain, excitement, compassion, and sympathy."

Gibbs also wrote, "If you fail to cultivate good relationships in your home, not only will your children and grandchildren reap a meager harvest, but any number of potential disasters await them, as they reap the ill whirlwind spun off by your actions and attitudes."

I (Pat) was out running one morning a couple of years ago, and I stopped at a Denny's restaurant to use the restroom. One of the employees was at the wash basin, shaving. He was a very chatty type and started sharing his life with me. He said, "Every time I shave, it reminds me of my father. I can still remember my dad shaving with a straight-edge razor. I guess I was about three or four. Then, when I was older, my dad taught me how to shave."

It made me think about how much our children learn from us, from simple things like shaving or putting on makeup to choosing a career or deciding what to believe about God.

Writing for *Newsweek,* Anna Quindlen says she wishes more people understood that "having children changes everything." She says, "There's constant grousing about the failure of various sports figures to serve as national role models, when all they are really qualified to do is pass a little ball around a little area. But the moment that little [umbilical] cord gets cut with those little scissors, two people have been turned into role models instantly, whether they like it or not."

Quindlen says too many men and women seem to think they can be good parents and still behave like irresponsible teenagers, and that's simply not the case. We agree with her that after you have children, "everything is a process of compromise and even self-sacrifice, or ought to be. The center has shifted, from sleeping late and midnight movies to Saturday soccer games and those night terrors that lead to three in a bed, two of them exhausted. This is all onerous. Clean up your act…. 'An inadvertent example' is how the psychologist Lawrence Balter describes what a parent becomes without even trying. A child is watching. And learning."

A friend named Laurie tells us that one of the important things she wants her children to learn is their responsibility toward the less fortunate. She says, "They need to learn to give and care for others around them."

She tells about getting her children involved in a ministry to the homeless on Christmas Eve. "We talked about what we were going to do days before it happened. The kids [ages five, seven, nine, and twelve] were just as excited as

I was.... The big night came and we all took the food we had prepared to church."

As it turned out, the parents didn't even get to serve the food because the children wanted to do it. "My seven-year-old was handing out bread, and we had to monitor him because he was giving out such generous servings that there would be none left for those at the end of the line."

She continues, "After the meal, while the dessert was being served, all the presents were handed out. A junior-high girl played carols on a piano, and we all sang together. I have a special memory of my oldest son standing arm-in-arm with a homeless man as they were singing and laughing together. My kids talk about this every Christmas. They want to do it again, and that is music to my ears."

Several years ago, when all our children were still at home, we spent Thanksgiving morning serving food at a homeless shelter in downtown Orlando. At first, the children weren't thrilled about going, but once we began serving, they really got into it. As we were leaving they all asked, "Can we do this again next year?" We did go back the next year and for several years after that. It was an experience the kids have never forgotten.

RESOLVE CONFLICT FAIRLY

A wise man (or woman) once said that anyone who has one child is a parent. But anyone who has two or more children is a referee. We can tell you from personal experience that this is true.

Proverbs 27:17 says, "As iron sharpens iron, so one man sharpens another." That's a pretty good description of life in our family! There is always plenty of iron sharpening iron, and that means there are also lots and lots of sparks. As the Bible points out, that's not necessarily bad. Difficulty in interpersonal relationships always provides an opportunity for growth.

We've sometimes taken comfort from the fact that Jesus Christ chose some very different personality types as his twelve apostles—his extended family during the years of his earthly ministry. These were not exactly the type of men Miss Manners would have seated at the same table during a dinner party.

For example, how well do you suppose Matthew got along with Simon the Zealot? Matthew was a Jew who collected taxes for the Roman government. In other words, he was an official representative of an occupying army. He was regarded as a traitor and hated by most of his fellow countrymen. Simon, on the other hand, was a member of a political group devoted to overthrowing the Romans by any means possible, including assassination and armed rebellion. From the Romans' point of view, he was a terrorist. Don't you imagine those two had some interesting discussions?

Or how about Peter and John? Peter was a man of action, an impulsive fellow who often acted first and then thought about it later, while John seems to have been a tender-hearted young man, a deep thinker who called himself "that disciple whom Jesus loved." Peter and John weren't exactly the sort of men who were naturally going to gravitate toward each other as best friends.

But Jesus knew exactly what he was doing when he chose those men to be his disciples. He knew they had the perfect qualities he was looking for to help him spread the good news of the kingdom.

Now, whenever we go through a time of conflict, we remind ourselves that God also knew what he was doing when he built our family. We don't think for a minute that it was our idea. He's the one who brought these children from all over the world to be our children. It helps to know that. But quite honestly, it can still be nerve-racking at times!

In a large, diverse family like ours, there's plenty of potential for conflict every day. Ruth and I do all we can to make relationships function smoothly. That doesn't mean we ignore conflicts or try to "stuff them." When conflict arises, as it inevitably does, we meet with all the parties involved and try to find the proper solution. We don't let disputes fester and grow into what the Bible calls a "bitter root" (Hebrews 12:15). We handle them as soon as we possibly can!

LOVE THEM ALL EQUALLY

It's tough being a parent in any situation, and it's especially tough if you're a parent in a family (like ours) where there are both birth children and adopted children. A survey of one hundred thousand children all over the world found that the number one thing children want from their parents is that all children receive equal affection.

That is so important. We would give one word of advice to those who may be considering adopting. Don't do it unless you are going to truly make that child your own: You cannot show favoritism to your birth child over the child you adopted.

Unless a child was adopted as an infant—and none of ours were—he is going to come into a family with some emotional baggage. The older a child is when adopted, the heavier his baggage is likely to be. And frankly, some of our kids have never been able to rid themselves of that old baggage. Most of our adopted children were once abused in some way—by their birth parents, by people who took advantage of them while they were living on the streets, or even by the orphanages where they lived.

Although we explained to our kids that it wasn't their fault that they were mistreated, that they didn't deserve the abuse that was heaped upon them, some of those old fears, doubts, and problems with self-esteem still remain.

It is very difficult to let go of something that has become a part of you even if that something hurts you. It's painful, but it's familiar, and that makes it almost comfortable after a while. Holding on to the regrets and hurts of the past is less frightening than setting them down and walking away from them.

With God's help, it is possible to help an adopted child overcome the hurts caused by an abusive past—but it takes an awful lot of love and effort. We have known some adopted children who were treated as second-class citizens in their new homes. They weren't given the same food, the same privileges, the same clothing, or the same love. That is a heartbreaking situation, and it is one that does not reflect an understanding that, as Christians, all of us are God's children by adoption. And he loves us so much that he was willing to send his own birth Son for us!

We've always done everything within our power to let our children know that we love them all equally. We also try to show them that our love is not conditional and that it is not diminished when they disobey us or come home with the weirdest haircut anyone has ever seen.

That doesn't mean that we treat all of them exactly the same. Children have different needs at different times in their lives, and we try to act accordingly. Today we may do something extra special for Gabi. Tomorrow it might be Alan's turn to get a special treat. We let our kids know that their turn will come, but that we simply cannot do the same things for everyone at the same time. Our rule is that we have always tried to do whatever is best for each individual child at the time, and we have always done it with love.

As you are making plans for educational opportunities, extracurricular activities, special events, or any other life events, all your children must be treated equally. The only differences in your treatment should be based upon their behavior, not their origin.

Equal treatment is also important in families where there are no adopted children. Children have different talents and personalities, and they should be given the opportunity to develop these traits in their own way. They will choose different routes. And some will move at a faster or slower pace than others. Regardless of their innate differences, each child has the right to be loved by her parents in the same way that her brothers and sisters are loved.

Our children have always absolutely loathed it whenever people compared them to each other. That's why we have made it a cardinal rule not to do so. When I (Pat) was growing up, my older sister, Carol, was an outstanding student, while I struggled academically. My mother invested hours to help me with my studies. Without her help, I might *still* be in high school! But despite my difficult time in school, I can't remember a time when my mother compared me to my sister. She never asked, "Why can't you get A's like Carol does?" She never made me feel bad that I didn't measure up to my sister academically. I appreciated her patience and understanding when I was a boy, and I have done my best to model that same behavior with my own children.

We've said it before, but it's so important that it bears repeating: Never ever compare your children with one another. It isn't good for anyone.

NEVER STOP LAUGHING

This may be one of the harder parenting challenges: You must maintain your sense of humor. Laughter helps. So laugh whenever you can!

Have you ever heard someone describing a difficult situation by saying, "I didn't know whether to laugh or cry"? If you are a parent, you are certainly going to run into plenty of occasions like that.

Take our advice and choose laughter over tears. Laughter is good for you. The Bible says, "A cheerful heart is good medicine" (Proverbs 17:22), and modern science has discovered that this is literally true. As author Herm Albright explains, "Laughing a hundred times a day yields the same cardiovascular workout as ten minutes of rowing. During a good belly laugh, your heart rate can top 120 beats a minute. So laugh it up! It's good for you!"

Over the years we've had lots of reasons to laugh. For example, there was the time Thomas took our van to school and then got a ride home with friends. He had absolutely no memory of driving to school even when he heard us calling the police to report that it had been stolen out of our driveway overnight.

It wasn't until Monday morning, when he saw the van sitting in his school's parking lot, that he remembered what he had done. A sense of humor came in handy when we had to call the police and tell them, "Guess what? Our van wasn't stolen after all."

Thomas is a brilliant student, but he sometimes reminds us of an absent-minded professor. As he himself once told us, "I know a lot. I just can't remember it." Ha!

When Thomas was a little boy, he was a good soccer player. However, in one game, he seemed to be having a terrible time on the field. He was stumbling around so badly that he looked as if he'd never been on a soccer field in his life.

After the game we found out why. On his way out of the house, he had grabbed his sister Sarah's shoes instead of his own. They were at least three sizes too small for him, yet he played the entire game in them. As you can imagine, his feet were pretty sore for a few days after that game. But that wasn't the end of it. Not long after that, he wore two left shoes to a game. He looked a little strange out there, but he actually performed pretty well. And we all got a good laugh out of it.

Another story began quite seriously but ended up with humor. Once Pat took the children to the beach for a couple of days over a long weekend. Thomas and his twin, Stephen, were running around on the beach one night, and Stephen ran full-speed ahead into a wooden post sticking out of the sand. He wasn't seriously injured, but he scared Thomas almost to death. Stephen was pretty bruised and battered. It was only after the swelling went down that we were able to laugh about what happened.

You see, Stephen is supposed to wear corrective lenses, but he didn't have them on the night the accident occurred. Besides that, he was wearing sunglasses—at night! No wonder he didn't see that board waiting to clobber him upside the head.

But probably the funniest thing about this incident came from Thomas. He was very worried about his brother's injuries, thinking that he might have a broken bone. He said to Pat, very seriously, "Dad, I'll get Stephen some milk."

"Milk?" Pat asked. "Why?"

"To build up his bones," Thomas replied. Pat had to struggle to keep from laughing. Thomas apparently thought he could infuse milk into Stephen's bones and make him "all better."

It really is true that kids do and say the "darndest" things sometimes. And it's fun and healthy to look back and have a good laugh.

Chapter 13

Four Things Every Child

Needs from Parents

Whatever the era, whatever the times, one thing will never change. Fathers and mothers, if you have children, they must come first. You must read to your children and you must hug your children and you must love your children. Your success as a family, our success as a society, depends not on what happens in the White House, but on what happens inside your house.

FORMER FIRST LADY BARBARA BUSH

Why is it easier to criticize what's wrong than it is to compliment what's right?

If you doubt that this is true, check out the letters to the editor in your local paper over the next few days. Most letters complain about something. People are much more likely to take action when they're angry or agitated. Think about it. If you go on a trip and the hotel is great, you probably won't give it another thought. But if the elevator is out of order or passing trains wake you up once an hour all night long—well, someone's going to get a long letter!

We have a feeling that most of us are like these letter writers when it comes to prayer. We have long lists of things we need to ask God for—the healing of someone who is sick, the protection of a child who is away from home, and so on. We don't often spend as much time thanking God for the good things he has given us as we do asking him to remove the things that trouble and threaten us.

Our point is simply this: It's a lot easier to see what our kids have done wrong than it is to see what they've done right. It's easier to complain about the bicycle that he left in the driveway than it is to remember to say, "Your room looks nice. Thanks for cleaning it up." It's easier to complain about the loud music coming out of her room than it is to say, "You're doing your homework, huh? That's great!" It's easier to complain about the C-minus in math than to congratulate him on the A in English.

This truth about human nature leads us to the four things every child needs from parents.

1. BE A CHEERLEADER

> I coach by encouragement.
> —Roy Williams, college basketball coach

Every child needs positive reinforcement from her parents. Without it, she will never become a responsible, capable adult. Dorothy Briggs writes, "Parents are like mirrors which reflect back to the child what he is like. Each child values himself to the degree that he has been valued. If the parent mirrors back to the child, 'I value you,' the child learns to value himself."

That's why we need to make it a point to look for the positive in our children's behavior and to affirm them when they do well and when they do the right and responsible thing. Pastor/author David Jeremiah writes, "James Dobson, the family expert who spent years studying adolescent behavior, once said in my presence, 'Here's the distilled wisdom of all my research. Here is what you need to do if you have adolescents: Just get them through it.'

"Just get them through it! Hang in there with them until the whitewater rapids of the teenage years are left behind."

Children—especially teenage children—may act disinterested and bored, as if they couldn't care less what anyone thought of them. But we have discovered that beneath that blasé facade, they really do care. It pleases them to know that you are pleased with them or with something they did. Everyone in the world, including our children, needs some affirmation and encouragement from time to time. As Proverbs 16:24 says, "Pleasant words are a honeycomb, sweet to the soul and healing to the bones." There's a lot of truth in those words.

One of the many things Pat is good at is complimenting me (Ruth) and the children. He looks for positive things he can bring up. We never leave the house to go out without Pat telling me, "You look great!" or "Wow! That's a great outfit." He does the same thing for our girls. I often hear him say, "Man, you're going to knock 'em dead today!" or "That color really brings out your eyes" or, one of their favorites, "Boy, you look several years older in that outfit." They love that one. You should see the big smiles that spread across their faces. (I do remind him he's going to have to switch that line in a few years.)

One of the greatest things any girl can hear from her father is a compliment. What her father says to her has a tremendous influence in shaping the way she sees herself. When I was a child, my father always whistled at my mother when she entered a room. He was always hugging her, kissing her, and telling her how wonderful she looked. Pat is the same way with our girls and me.

And he is forever patting the boys on the back and saying things like "Hey, good-looking" or "Boy, you're growing up to be a good-looking young man." Sometimes they act as if they don't appreciate it, but I can tell they do, even if it embarrasses them a little bit. A compliment like that, coming from their father, means so much! They even look taller because they stand up straighter when their dad compliments them.

It doesn't take a lot to encourage your children and help them feel good about themselves. You just have to look for opportunities to arise and then take advantage of them when they do. Recently, as I (Ruth) was driving Kati, Alan, and Gabi to school, Kati asked Gabi, "Did you remember your study guide for history?"

"Yep," Gabi answered. "Right here."

"Good," Kati smiled. "I didn't want to see you lose points on the test for not having it."

"Kati," I said, "that was very thoughtful of you." Kati beamed, buoyed all day by the fact that her mom had told her she was thoughtful.

Another time, when Alan and Kati were arguing, Gabi helped them negotiate a settlement. When they told Ruth that their sister had helped them find a solution to their problem, Ruth said, "Gabi, thank you for being so mature." Again Gabi's entire countenance brightened from that one simple compliment.

And then there's the sweet elderly lady who sits about two rows in front of us at church every Sunday morning. She is hard of hearing and uses a walker to get around. She always leaves the service just a few minutes early so she won't get run over by the crowd when the final benediction is pronounced. A friendly man and his wife sit behind her almost every Sunday, and the gentleman usually helps her get up and start moving in the right direction.

One Sunday morning that helpful couple was not in church. So, as the little lady got up to leave, Alan stepped out of our pew and helped her get started. When he returned to our pew, I (Pat) gave him a high-five, while Ruth hugged him and told him how proud she was that he had been so kind. Alan went through his day with the pride and pleasure that come from knowing you've done a good thing.

These are just a few examples of how parents can build a child's self-esteem and character at the same time. Sometimes, when the kids get mad at Pat because he is disciplining them, I (Ruth) say, "I know you don't see it now, but you have the best dad in the world. He loves you so much that he's willing for you to be mad at him now. He wants you to learn from this so you'll grow up to be happy and successful."

David, one of our Filipino sons, graduated from high school in 1998. Two weeks later, he started summer college classes, but he was not ready for the level of work and focus it required. He came home three weeks later and said, "Dad, I don't want to do this."

Not long after that, David went into the marine recruiting office and enlisted. Soon he was on a bus heading to Paris Island, South Carolina, for twelve weeks of basic training. And he thought college was hard! It was twelve weeks of the most grueling physical work he had ever been through—and without any contact with home—not even a phone call.

At the end of his training in November 1998, we went up to Paris Island for his graduation ceremony on the parade grounds. It was a powerful, emotional experience to see all those young men and women in uniform, all the flags flying and bands blaring and officers saluting.

After the ceremony ended, the young people and their parents all rushed out to the parade grounds to greet each other. With tears streaming down his face, David ran up to Pat, gave him a huge hug. "Dad," he said through tears, "I heard your voice. I didn't quit."

Today, David is happily married, is still a marine, and doesn't quit.

Pat has always encouraged the children to "stick with it," to never give up. Many times over the years, they have said, "Dad, okay, we get it." They sometimes get tired of hearing it, but when they need it, Pat's voice is in their heads, encouraging them, cheering them on.

Another tip for cheering on our children comes from writer Haim Ginott: "Treat a child as though he is already the person he's capable of becoming." What a wonderful way to help your child fulfill his God-given potential and grow into a capable, responsible adult! We call it *the vision thing*. That phrase means helping your children catch a vision of their successful future.

Jerrod M. Post, a Washington DC psychiatrist, has studied and profiled Saddam Hussein for the CIA. He said, "He has always compensated for a wounded psychology, which was more like the empty hole in the ground where he was found."

Post then added, "Starting at age nine Saddam's uncle filled him with dreams of glory and told him he would be inscribed in the history of Iraq and Arab nationalism. He came to believe he was destined for greatness as a major world leader." What a sad story about a misdirected life that could have turned out so differently if Saddam had had the right influences as a young boy.

Our son Alan has just finished high school, and he's not interested in going to college, so we've been talking to him about joining the military. We tell him how good he's going to look in his military uniform, how proud of him we're going to be, and so on. We're not making any of this up. We really mean what we say. But we're also trying to paint a picture in Alan's mind. We want him to see himself wearing an officer's uniform someday, to have that vision of a successful future.

During the 2003 season, our son Bobby was the hitting coach for the Cincinnati Reds Rookie League team in Sarasota, Florida. I (Pat) always tell Bobby that when he's working with his young players, he should say things like, "Now, when you get to the big leagues…" or "In a few years, when you're facing major-league pitching…" When Bobby drops comments like that into his casual conversation, he'll be helping those young players believe that they have the ability to make it to the major leagues. As a result, they'll have more confidence in themselves, and they'll try harder to learn what Bobby is trying to teach them.

By the way, I do the same thing with Bobby. When difficult situations arise, I say, "Bobby, how are you going to handle a situation like this when you're the general manager of a major league team?" We are convinced that Bobby has the ability to become a major league GM someday. I just want to help by enabling him to see himself in that position.

2. GIVE CHILDREN THE TIME THEY NEED

> My father worked two jobs and was often absent. This was an invaluable lesson for me when I became a father. I realized how much just being there means.
>
> —Tim Russert, journalist

Two of Pat's favorite professional basketball players retired in 2003. One was Michael Jordan. The other was the San Antonio Spurs' David Robinson. Most everyone knows a lot about Michael, but David probably did not get the attention he deserved. Of course he was an excellent player. David helped the Spurs win NBA championships in 1999 and 2003, but that's not really why Pat likes him so much. What Pat likes about David Robinson can best be seen by an account of what he was doing in the locker room shortly after the championship game in 1999, while reporters and cameramen waited patiently off to the side: He was teaching his son how to tie a necktie. According to Phil Taylor, writing in *Sports Illustrated*, the scene played out like this:

> "How do you tie a tie, Daddy?" asked David Jr., six years old at the time.
>
> "Well, you bring this part around here and tuck this in here, and then you pull down here," Robinson answered softly, as he performed each step.
>
> "Is it hard?" David Jr. asked.
>
> "Not once you know how to do it," said his father. "Don't worry. I'll teach you."
>
> They went on like that for a few minutes, a father chatting with his son as though they were the only two people in the room. On the night that he reached the peak of his profession, Robinson was content to be David Jr.'s dad, which should come as no surprise to anyone who followed him during his four seasons at the Naval Academy or since he joined the San Antonio Spurs in 1989. Robinson has often been called an extraordinary man, but in truth he is an ordinary one, in the best sense.

Author Ray Pelletier, whom we quoted at the beginning of this section, says that time is one of the most important ingredients necessary for the construction of well-adjusted and responsible children. He writes that when it comes to time, "Your children need as much of it as you can give. For example, they need a period of uninterrupted time with you when you come home from work. They know you're busy and exhausted. They can see it. But now you're home, and they need to know that they're a priority."

He adds, "They need that daily dose of security. They need you to listen to them. They need to know you're interested in what's going on in their lives. They know you've got your mind on a lot of other things.... But they want to feel they're as important to you as all those 'other things.' It's not too much to ask. Their feelings and needs aren't a burden to you. They're your children."

Giving your children time means being available to them when they need you. It means letting them know that they are a very high priority in your life, subordinate only to your relationship with God and your relationship with your spouse. Your kids should also understand that, even though your job is not as important to you as they are, it *is* important, and you can't *always* set it aside to tend to their smallest need.

But they should also feel that you will do your absolute best to put other matters aside and listen when they really feel the need to have your attention. Remember Lucy's psychiatrist office in *Peanuts?* She has a little sign that says, "The doctor is in." Your children should feel that Mom (or Dad) "is always in."

Pat and I (Ruth) travel for business. It's something we've both always done—something that comes with our careers. Yet we are "always in." Many times I get calls on my voicemail saying, "Mommy, call me. I have something to tell you." I always call at night to see how things are going, and I can hear the kids' excitement as we talk over the phone. I get to give advice and encouragement, and I almost always hear one of the kids say, "Mom, thanks for calling and talking to me. Can we talk more about it when you get home?" Of course!

One of the things I like about such conversations is that they give me the opportunity to be proactive and to teach my children to be the same. We both have time to consider possible alternatives and then have a meaningful discussion when I return. Many times, when someone hits us with a request in person, we tend to give reactive responses. But when there's more time to think about a problem, we're much more likely to come up with a responsible solution. In fact, sometimes when I'm home, we'll set aside a day or two to think something through.

It has been said that in order to be in your children's memories tomorrow, it is necessary to be in their lives today. Clinical psychologist Dr. Wade Horn, director of the National Fatherhood Initiative, says that before any man can truly call himself a father, he has to understand the meaning of three important words: *time, commitment,* and *responsibility.*

In his best-selling book *Always Daddy's Girl,* psychologist/author H. Norman Wright says that one of the greatest things any dad can do for his daughter is to be approachable. "Approachability involves communication at a level where your dad is open, nondefensive, interested and responsive," he writes. He goes on to say that "approachable fathers listen, carefully, to what a daughter may have difficulty verbalizing. He listens—not only with his ears—but with his eyes and heart as well." Although Dr. Wright is speaking specifically about the father-daughter relationship, we believe that what he says applies across the board to parents and children of both genders.

Giving your children time means giving them a chance to think things through with you and to express themselves on subjects that are important to them. Parents whose conversations with their kids consist of a ten-minute lecture are not really spending time with their children. A lecture is a monologue, one person speaking and the other listening. There are appropriate times for lectures, but what children also need from their parents are two-way conversations—dialogue.

At the dinner table not too long ago, we were having a discussion about life in general: school, friends, news stories, and so forth. You never know what will come up in a conversation like that, but you can be certain that it will be interesting. As the discussion heated up, Pat began "lecturing" on some subject, probably something he saw in the newspaper. Through the years, all the kids have teased Pat about his lectures, a style which undoubtedly comes from his being a professional speaker. He tends to get into the lecturing mode almost naturally.

Now, our Kati is a special child. Kati, who turned eighteen last August, was adopted out of a Romanian orphanage when she was five years old. Tragically, she was one of those children who were literally caged in their cribs for years without much of anything in the way of stimulation, attention, or love. As a result of her early deprivation, Kati has had some learning challenges. It is sometimes difficult for her to express what she's thinking, and she can use words in very creative ways. On this particular evening, as Pat moved into high gear, Kati interrupted him with, "Dad, you know what? You need to be more of a casual dad."

There was dead silence at the table for a moment until Pat asked, "Kati, what do you mean by 'casual dad'?"

"You know," she said, "just talk and let us talk and maybe not say anything. Just listen to us."

Pat laughed and said, "You know, Kati, you're right. I've been talking too much, so let's hear what you think."

What a good reminder of the importance of taking the time to listen to what our children are thinking. Comedian Bill Cosby, who also has a doctorate in education, was asked why he has such good rapport with children. "Because I understand them," he replied. "When I talk to them, I give them a chance to think and answer. Many adults don't have the patience for that."

Theologian and author Frederick Buechner says, "You can't be too careful what you tell a child because you never know what he'll take hold of and spend the rest of his life remembering you by." In the same way, you may never know how much a few minutes of your time will impact your child's life—or how long she will remember and treasure those few moments with you or how long he will be guided and inspired by the advice you gave during your brief time together.

3. LET CHILDREN BE RESPONSIBLE

> Where parents do too much for their children, the children will not do much for themselves.
> —Elbert Hubbard

Our children need for us to step back and let them experience the consequences of their own actions. This is a lot harder than it sounds.

It hurts to watch your child suffer even if the pain is caused by something she did. Most parents have a natural tendency to want to step in and fix things, to make everything all right. But even though that might stop the pain for a little while, it won't build character for the long haul. In fact, your action might make their behavior worse the next time there's a problem.

A woman named Pauline told us how hard it was for her to let her daughter, Diana, get a failing grade on a term paper. The girl had known about the project for several weeks but kept putting it off. Whenever Pauline asked her how the paper was coming along, Diana had said, "I've got plenty of time," "Don't worry about it," or something similar.

Thus, at eight o'clock the Sunday night before the paper was due, Diana had only five pages written. Her room was a jumble of books and notebooks. By this time Diana's nonchalant attitude had been replaced by out-and-out panic.

"I'll never get this done in time," she whined. "Why did I put it off so long?"

Pauline told us that her inclination was to get in there and start helping. She was a much faster typist than Diana was, and she was pretty good with words. Maybe Diana could give Mom the gist of what she wanted to say, and Mom could put it into proper language.

But then Pauline thought about all the times she had tried unsuccessfully to get Diana moving on the project. And she remembered other times when she'd turned into Supermom at the last minute, rescuing her child from impending disaster. As hard as it was, she decided that this time she would have to let her daughter reap the consequences of her procrastination. At 10:30, when Pauline went to bed, Diana was still at her computer keyboard, still panicked, and still a long, long way from the finish line.

Diana finally finished her paper about 2:00 a.m., and it showed. Her paper received an F grade, but she learned a valuable lesson about responsibility that will stay with her the rest of her life. Way to go, Pauline!

We agree with an article in *Our Daily Bread Devotional* that says, "Loving parents long to protect their children from unnecessary pain, but wise parents know the danger of over-protection. They know that the freedom to choose is at the heart of what it means to be human, and that a world without choice would be worse than a world without pain."

Another way you can teach your children to be responsible is to let them do things for themselves. Stand back and let them fail if they haven't put forth the effort necessary to succeed. Help them with tasks when they really need your help, sure. But don't do everything *for* them, or they'll never learn to do anything! Here's what Irene Daria, writing in *Parents Magazine,* has to say:

> Five- and-six-year-olds can and should do regular chores. Assuming more responsibility at home is as crucial for children as learning to read, being physically active and making friends. Children this age are better able to concentrate on a specific activity than they were earlier. They're more adept with their hands and less likely to be discouraged by small setbacks. They have a sincere desire to please and are proud of their accomplishments.

Daria says that allowing kids to help out around the house makes them feel "independent, competent, and important with their family."

Derrick Brooks, one of the key players with the Tampa Bay Buccaneers, 2003 Super Bowl Champions, is widely regarded as one of the nicest guys in pro football. Good parenting may be one reason why. Brooks told *USA Today* reporter Jarrett Bell that in grade school he was the class clown. "I'd crack jokes, shoot staples, flick bubblegum. I did it all."

One day when he was in fifth grade—and right in the middle of his clown act—Brooks was surprised when his stepfather, A. J. Mitchell, opened the door and strode into the classroom. Mitchell, who had been watching through a back window, grabbed his stepson out of his seat, dragged him to the front of the room, and gave him a good spanking in front of his classmates.

"He gave me ten or fifteen good licks," Brooks told Bell. "I ran all the way home, about two miles. He had warned me, 'If you're a clown, I'll come up there and be a bigger fool than you.' But I didn't think he'd take the time to leave work to do that. As I got older, I started to see what that message was all about: If you don't have the right foundation, you're going to crack and crumble."

Brooks remembers that the spanking from his stepfather wasn't where the lesson ended. His dad also pulled him off the school football team.

"If I'm not there, the team is going to lose," Brooks protested.

"Exactly," his dad said. "And you can tell them why: It's because you didn't learn to respect authority and treat people the way they deserve to be treated."

"Thank God I had parents who cared," Brooks says now.

Fisher DeBerry, head football coach for the Air Force Academy, says he doesn't quite believe it when he hears people talking about how tough it is to be a kid today. He says, "I remember having to work at a young age. I remember never having any downtime to play video games, worry about dying my hair and getting body piercings, or watching television for hours and hours a day."

He goes on, "The only reason it's tougher to be a kid nowadays is because parents have made it easier to shirk responsibility and, more importantly, accountability. Kids don't do chores. They get a car when they turn sixteen. If you are forking over twenty bucks to your children today, they're going to be expecting twenty more next week and fifty next year. We're not making the kids work for it. That leaves the child with no sense of accountability and no appreciation for what money truly represents. Money is earned through hard work."

Tough words? Certainly. But words worth hearing.

4. Give Children a Sense of Belonging

> The home is the natural habitat for growing human beings and shaping eternal souls.
>
> —Gloria Gaither, singer/composer

If a child doesn't feel as if he belongs, terrible things can happen to her. This morning's newspaper has another story about a drive-by shooting. A fifteen-year-old boy, standing in front of a friend's house in the middle of the afternoon, was hit by two shots fired from a passing car. It was no surprise to read that police are calling the shooting gang-related. Fortunately, in this instance, the victim was not seriously injured.

What makes teenagers join gangs? Why would anyone with an ounce of intelligence want to get involved in an organization that will put his life in constant jeopardy or force him to participate in violence that could send him to prison for the rest of his life?

There may be many answers to that question. But sociologists tell us that the most important one is this: Joining a gang gives young men (or women) a sense of belonging that they would not otherwise have. Some teenagers (and even preteenagers) join gangs for the same reason that other kids get swept into cults headed by spiritual dictators like Korea's Sun Myung Moon.

Teenagers need to belong, and the best thing they can belong to is a loving family.

Even though our teenage children may sometimes act as if they don't want anything to do with us, that's not really true. Research undertaken by Ohio State University professor Stephen Gavazzi showed, "Kids need to feel a strong sense of belonging to a family. At the same time, there has to be a fostered sense of individuality that comes within a relationship." The researchers say that it is a myth to think that we no longer have an impact on our children once they become teenagers. "If parents give up, that's when the real trouble starts," they write.

They go on to say that teenagers who are sure of their parents' love, and whose parents "are reasonable" in their decision making, have a greater sense of well-being and of identification with their parents. "Peers are not a signifi-cant influence in any part of a teenager's life, other than in terms of what clothes they wear or how they wear their hair. Only when the family doesn't operate at adequate levels—establishing the connectedness and individuality—does peer influence take over. The bottom line is that the earlier you start doing positive things in a child's life, the better off you are going to be." Too many times, children feel as if they are not really partners in the family, as if they are on the outside looking in.

Albert Lewis II knows all about the importance of belonging to a strong, supportive family. When Albert was just eighteen months old, he fell from a fourth-floor window in his hometown of Riverdale, Georgia. Miraculously he survived, but his emotional and mental development seemed to be affected by his injuries. He was diagnosed with infantile autism and developmental delays, and experts told his parents that he should be placed in a school for children with learning disabilities.

But Albert's parents refused to treat him as if he were different or slower than other children. They loved him, encouraged him, and instilled in him a sense of strength and belonging.

The first few years of school were a struggle for Albert, but thanks to the patience of his teachers and the encouragement of his parents, he eventually began to catch up. Eventually he found himself in a program for gifted students; he was named a National Ventures Scholar and Outstanding Cadet in the Southeastern Cadet Leadership Program. For the last two years he has been named to *Who's Who Among American High-School Students.* He is active in his church's teen ministry. He also has been an outstanding member of Riverdale High School's track, wrestling, and football teams. He even earned a spot on the all-area football team.

Not bad for a kid who didn't "belong" in a school with his peers. Clearly he knew he belonged to God and his family. Let us explain. The Old Testament book of Ruth tells about a great miracle that arose from having a sense of belonging. In this case it was not a son or daughter who felt that she belonged; rather, it was a daughter-in-law, Ruth, the woman who gave the book its name.

Ruth lived in the country of Moab, where she was married to the son of a Jewish widow named Naomi. After both their husbands had died, Naomi decided to return to her hometown of Bethlehem, and she suggested to her daughter-in-law that she go home to her own people.

"May the LORD show kindness to you," Naomi said, "as you have shown kindness to [my son] and to me. May the LORD grant that...you will find rest in the home of another husband" (Ruth 1:8-9).

Ruth wouldn't hear of it: "Don't urge me to leave you or to turn back from you," she said. "Where you go I will go, and where you stay I will stay. Your people will be my people and your God my God. Where you die I will die, and there I will be buried. May the LORD deal with me, be it ever so severely, if anything but death separates you and me" (verses 16-17).

Why did Ruth insist on going to live in a foreign land with her mother-in-law? She loved Naomi, and apparently her love for her mother-in-law made her feel as though she belonged to Naomi's family. Because of Naomi, she was ready to go "home" to a country she'd never even visited rather than stay in her native land with her own family. And so "When Naomi realized that Ruth was determined to go with her, she stopped urging her [to go back to her own people]" (verse 18).

As it turned out Ruth married one of Naomi's relatives, a man named Boaz. But that's not where the story ends. If you turn over to the first chapter of Matthew, you'll find Ruth listed in the genealogy of Jesus Christ. Ruth was not a Jew. She had grown up in a country and culture that worshiped false gods. Yet as a member of Naomi's family, she became the grandmother of Israel's great King David and thus an integral member of the family tree that resulted in the birth of the Messiah.

How would world history have been different if Ruth had not experienced that sense of belonging with Naomi and her family?

We can only hope that our example, love, time, and encouragement will lead to good, responsible actions from our children. We do know for certain that all the investments we've made in our twins, Stephen and Thomas, have paid off many times over.

These two young men, our most recent college graduates, have always been model children. They always followed the rules and listened to our advice. In fact, neither one will make a major decision without first discussing it with us to get our point of view. In college they studied hard and made the dean's list. At each stage of life, they proved themselves worthy to move to the next level.

Stephen and Thomas have been pure treasures. They are proof that parenting can be a joyful, rewarding experience. But poet Dan Baker reminds us that if we love our children, we must not simply sing them our song. Instead, we must follow their guidance:

Teach me to sing,
for, when I am alone,
I will need the melody.

We simply have to teach our children to sing.

Chapter 14

HELPING YOUR CHILDREN
DISCOVER THE JOY OF HARD WORK

The harder I work, the more I live.
GEORGE BERNARD SHAW

It's four o'clock on a lazy Saturday afternoon. Thirteen-year-old Joey is sitting on the bed in his room, strumming tunelessly on his guitar. In the background, on the television on his dresser, Bugs Bunny is making a fool of Elmer Fudd for what must be the ten thousandth time. Of course, if you asked Joey, he'd tell you that he's not really watching cartoons. He's much too old. He was just channel surfing, and this is where he "happened" to land.

Through his opened door, Joey sees his mom walk past with a bucket full of cleaning supplies and head into the hall bathroom. Joey keeps strumming on his guitar.

Ten or fifteen minutes later, Mom comes out of the bathroom, her brow glistening with perspiration, and trudges down the stairs. Joey hears the vacuum roar to life, but again he doesn't budge from his guitar and his cartoon.

After she's finished vacuuming, Mom comes back up the stairs, this time with a basketful of laundry that needs to be folded. On her way into the master bedroom, she stops and stands in the doorway of Joey's room.

"Joey?"

He keeps on strumming. "Yeah?"

"Would you mind taking out the trash for me?" she asks.

Joey sighs and gently sets his guitar on his bed. "Okay, Mom," he says, but his voice and the expression on his face tell her that even though he'll do what she asked, he's not too happy about it.

As he goes to take out the trash, he mumbles under his breath, "All I ever do around here is work!" He says this even though he's been sitting in his room for the last hour and a half doing absolutely nothing! And this scene is repeated thousands of times, perhaps even millions of times, every single day in American homes where teenagers reside.

You see, many teenagers think they are working hard when they're not. Left to themselves, kids just want to "chill" and "veg." They don't know what hard work is. Thus, one of the most important things parents can do for their children is to introduce them to the value of working hard. We must teach them that the things they want in life will not simply fall into their laps, but must be worked for. A child who is allowed to chill and veg all of the time will likely grow up to become a cold cucumber instead of a mature adult.

In the Williams household, children are expected to keep their rooms neat, put their laundry away, tidy up their bathrooms, and tend to their own clothing or sporting equipment. Do they always do it? Of course not. But we continually encourage our kids to raise their own expectations of themselves, and we try to model, by our own actions, what we expect them to do.

Do our children like doing chores? No way! They often balk, gripe, or cut corners. Think about it. So do you! We don't want to give you the wrong idea. They're great kids. They generally have helpful, positive attitudes, and they do their jobs right most of the time. But kids are kids. They'll slack off a bit or sweep the dirt under the rug if you don't encourage standards of excellence.

Getting kids to work hard can be hard work in and of itself. But it's worth it. Not because it produces squeaky-clean floors and windowpanes, but because hard work builds character and strength of spirit.

Nine Things Every Teenager Ought to Know

Billionaire Bill Gates made news when he gave a tell-it-like-it-is speech to a group of high-school seniors. Gates didn't hold back. He doesn't think high school is preparing today's teenagers for the real world, and he told them so.

Well, nobody wants to be the bearer of bad news. But the truth is that what Gates told those teenagers is true: Life is not always fair. Your future employer will probably expect you to start at the bottom and work your way up the ladder…and your boss is likely to make the toughest teacher you ever had seem like a sweetheart. Today's teenagers definitely need a dose of such reality.

But they need something else, too. They need to know that faith in Christ will get them through all situations and enable them to become more than they ever thought they could be. But Bill Gates got us to thinking, so with a tip of the hat to him, here is our list of "Nine Things Every Teenager Ought to Know."

1. Sometimes Life's Not Fair

That shouldn't be a surprise to anyone, yet one of the most common complaints from teenagers is, "That's not fair." Jesus warned us in John 16:33 that we will have tribulation in this world. He never promised us a pain-free life. But he told us that when the world gets us down, we can still rejoice because he has overcome the world! Life isn't always fair. Some people get lucky bounces they don't deserve. Others get bad breaks they also don't deserve. We parents need to make sure our kids understand that anyone who wants to succeed in life must learn to roll with life's punches and keep on moving toward the goal. God is in control, and he is working everything—even the bad times—together for our good (see Romans 8:28).

2. There's Nothing Quite So Annoying As Misplaced Self-Confidence

The Bible says that we (and our children) should all be careful about having an inflated view of ourselves (see Romans 12:3). It is important for our children to have a healthy sense of self-respect, but if their self-confidence crosses the line into arrogance, they'll turn people off—especially if they're new on the job. As Gates puts it, "The real world expects you to accomplish something genuine before you feel good about yourself."

3. It's Important to Be Faithful in the Little Things

Our teenagers may be disappointed when they find out what jobs are paying these days. In the real world you almost always have to start at the bottom, and entry-level salaries or hourly wages aren't usually the ticket to the car, clothes, or home of your dreams. But Jesus said that those who prove themselves faithful in small matters will be given greater and greater responsibilities. That's true in the spiritual realm as well as the corporate world. Our teens must understand that it is only when they have proven faithful in the little matters that they can graduate to the bigger ones.

4. Be Nice to Nerds, Geeks, and Dweebs—You May End Up Working for One!

Once our kids have graduated from high school, they are likely to find that the definition of who's popular and who's not shifts dramatically. In the "real world" you can't get by on a bright smile or beautiful eyes and hair. Out there it's what you *know* that counts.

We've mentioned that our son Thomas is attending graduate school at Seton Hall University; he's working on an MBA and a master's in sports administration. Thomas is our "brain child," the one with the 4.2 grade point average. Studying is just his thing, and he works really hard. Before he went off to get his undergraduate degree at the University of Florida, he was the one we called whenever we had a computer question. He was also on the baseball, soccer, and swimming teams in high school, so he's not the kind of person others might call a geek or a nerd. However, because he is *so* smart, one of the standing jokes around our house goes like this: "You'd better be nice to Thomas. We'll all be working for him one day."

It's true. Those who spend their high school and college years studying instead of partying are usually the ones who wind up in charge. No wonder the book of Proverbs tells us that "fools despise wisdom and instruction" (1:7, NASB). We have taught our kids to listen to what the Bible has to say about wisdom: "Exalt her, and she will promote you; she will bring you honor, when you embrace her. She will place on your head an ornament of grace; a crown of glory she will deliver to you" (Proverbs 4:8-9, NKJV).

5. It's Okay to Say, "Do You Want Fries with That?"

The Bible says that having a job—any honest job—is a badge of honor. Wouldn't it be a great world if every teenager understood that it is much more dignified to work at a fast-food joint than to spend his time sponging off his parents (or the government) while he looks for the perfect job?

6. If You Mess Up, Don't Try to Blame Someone Else

Finger-pointing is a very human tendency, but we let our kids know early on that it won't get them anywhere. Way back in the Garden of Eden, Adam blamed Eve for making him eat the forbidden fruit. Then Eve turned around and blamed the serpent.

In today's society it seems that most people are looking to blame someone else whenever anything goes wrong. The truth is that everybody makes mistakes from time to time. Everybody messes up. Someone has said that it's not a disgrace to fall, unless you just lie there and never get up. Instead, learn from your mistakes. Then pick yourself up, dust yourself off, and get back in the race!

7. When It Comes to Tough, You Ain't Seen Nothin' Yet

Have your kids had some tough teachers in school? Have they been stuck with teachers who demanded too much or who didn't grade fairly? Well, maybe it's a good time to let your teens know that things are even tougher out there in the working world.

Gabi found a new job assisting in a beauty salon. In a job market where it was almost impossible for a teenager to get a summer job, she was very fortunate. In fact, the June 9, 2003, issue of *USA Today* said that the unemployment rate for teens in the work force stood at 18.5 percent, the highest level in nine years. The rate is so high because teenagers are "being forced to compete with new college grads who are jobless, current college students who can't find paid internships, and even laid-off adults" for what used to be easy-to-get summer jobs.

Despite Gabi's good fortune, she came home one day and announced, "My boss is mean."

"What do you mean by *mean?*" we asked.

"She gives orders and wants it done really fast," she said.

Imagine that! A boss giving orders and expecting to have them followed—quickly! Welcome to the real world, Gabi! A boss is much tougher than a teacher because she has to make a profit. Her job depends on it. Anyone who doesn't contribute to the achievement of that goal won't be around very long.

Jesus said that anyone who does not "bear fruit" is good for nothing except being cut down and thrown into the fire (see John 15:6). That's the way it works in the "real world." Those who do not bear fruit are going to have a difficult time hanging on to a job. We've always advised our children not to avoid the tough, demanding teachers. They are the ones who will prepare their students for life after graduation.

8. What? No Summer Vacation?

If your teenagers complain about how hard they're working, it might be a good time to tell them that, in the real world, they won't get three months off for vacation every year. Nor will they get two weeks at Christmas and another week for spring break. But that's all right. Hard work won't kill them; it will make them stronger.

This may seem harsh, but in our house, no one gets the entire summer "off." They either go to swim camp, tennis camp, Bible camp, or summer school—or they work. We do take a couple of trips as a family during the summer, but no one gets a solid three-month break. Can you imagine a summer with nineteen kids hanging around the house? No way!

We've always gotten our children involved in something for the summer. We only had four at home full-time during the summer of 2003. Gabi and

Caroline worked. Kati was in summer school and went to swim camp, and Alan spent six weeks in his native country (Brazil) working at a church mission.

Would our kids rather just take it easy and lie around for three months? Of course! They are, after all, teenagers. Even so, after a two-week break at the beginning of the summer, they are restless and in need of stimulation, so we always plan a full summer for them. We want them to have fun, but we also want them to be involved and—hopefully—learning something.

9. Yes, There Are Winners and Losers in Life

We have tried to build a society which acknowledges that all human beings have the same inherent dignity and worth. And that's good.

But in some instances we've gone so far as to make it appear that there are no winners and losers in life—and that's bad. You see, there is such a thing as right behavior as opposed to wrong behavior. There are right answers as opposed to wrong answers. It does matter what you do. Hard work pays off with promotions, raises, and a good reputation. Those who slack off and try to coast through their careers are likely to find themselves standing in the unemployment line.

YOU'RE NEVER TOO YOUNG

When should you start teaching your children about the importance of hard work? Early. Consider this:

- **Mozart** wrote his first minuet at the age of five and had completed his first opera by the time he was nine.
- **Ray Charles** started playing the piano when he was three.
- Rock singer **Jewell** joined her dad's singing act when she was six, making up songs on the spot.
- **Buddy Holly** won a talent show at the age of five by singing "Down the River of Memories."
- **Chopin** gave his first public performance at the age of eight.

- **George Harrison** was fourteen when he joined John Lennon and Paul McCartney in their band.
- The artist formerly known as **Prince** taught himself to play the piano when he was seven.

In his book *Emotional Intelligence,* Daniel Goleman writes, "At the 1992 Olympics, twelve-year-old members of the Chinese diving team had put in as many total lifetime practice dives as had members of the American team in their early twenties.... The violin virtuosos of the twentieth century began studying their instrument at around five; international chess champions started on the game at an average age of seven, while those who rose only to national prominence started at ten."

You're never too young (or too old) to do great things.

ENCOURAGE YOUR CHILDREN

One thing we have stressed over and over again in this book—and we've done so on purpose—is the importance of encouraging our children. It would be very difficult to overstate the role encouragement plays in the growth process from child to successful adult. Part of encouraging is helping children find satisfaction in their achievements.

We believe that it is vitally important for us to stand by and support every one of our children. But we strive not to do too much for them or to be overprotective. When you show support for your child, it tells him, "I believe in you, and I'm here to give you a hand if you need one." Acting overly protective tells a child, "I'm afraid you can't make it on your own. That's why I have to do things for you."

Case in point. Several years ago a young man was drafted in the first round by a major league baseball team. Talk was that this kid had "star" written all over him. He was expected to be someone who could turn a team around with his bat and glove. But instead he's been languishing in the lower levels of the minor leagues for several years, and he's never shown anywhere near the level of play that was expected of him. It's growing more unlikely every day that he's ever going to make it as a major league player.

It's difficult to say what went wrong. But we keep hearing that his parents were way too protective. For example, every time he made a move from one team to another, from one city to another, they moved right along with him. At the end of every game, instead of hanging out with his teammates, he went home with Mom and Dad.

Finally, a couple of years ago, he got tired of that and told his parents he wasn't going to live with them anymore. That led to an argument, and now we hear that he's going through something of a rebellious state. He's traded in his clean-cut all-American-boy image for somewhere around twenty-six tattoos all over his body. He's not performing well on the field because he has "issues."

It's too bad Mom and Dad didn't understand that a parent's job is not only to give their children roots, but wings as well. We have to show them we care enough about them to want them to be able to fly off on their own someday. If our children are afraid to leave the nest, then we haven't done our job.

When a child is overprotected, he may come to feel that his parents don't have much faith in him. But the truth is that every child is full of God-given potential. And parents can help kids believe that. For example, as a young boy, Thomas was an above-average swimmer, and we always encouraged him in that sport.

Once, just before a race began, an official asked Thomas, "Are you going to win?"

"Yes," came the reply.

"How do you know?" the man asked.

"Because my father told me I can," Thomas explained.

This illustrates the fact that children are likely to see themselves through their parents' eyes. Thomas saw himself as a winner that day and today. He is definitely a winner in all areas of life.

Of course we are proud of all of our kids, no matter whether they finish first in the race or last. Whether they succeed or fail, the important thing is that they have dreams and that they pursue those dreams with confidence. As Charles Swindoll writes:

> Do you have a child who is mechanically inclined? He (or she) needs to know you notice. Make comments about it. Brag on their ability. Do you have a child who is athletic and well-coordinated? He needs to know you believe he is well-coordinated. You say, "That's obvious." But perhaps he hasn't heard it directly from you. He wants to hear you say it.... You have a child who is intellectually gifted? You sense that she would be good at research, probing deeply into various subjects? Mention the future possibilities. Help her find the right university. Rather than hammering away on petty stuff that doesn't matter, spend more time discovering how your children's interests can be channeled.

Doing as Swindoll suggests is a great way to help build your children's self-esteem. It's also a great way to help them determine their future careers.

Another way you can encourage your children to work hard, and thus succeed in life, is to work right alongside them. For example, a few years ago in the community of Riverdale, New York, a school bookstore sold far more textbooks than there were students in the entire school. An investigation revealed the reason: Asian American families were buying two sets of textbooks—one for the child and another for the parents. That way parents could learn the lessons right along with their child and be better prepared to help their children succeed in school. Reflecting on this story in his book, *The De-Valuing of America*, former Secretary of Education William Bennett said, "The scholastic success of many Asian American children has reminded us all of the importance of parental involvement."

Do you ever wonder why there are so many amazing rags-to-riches stories involving Asian Americans? They came here only a generation ago with almost nothing and barely speaking English, but they have quickly become prosperous, prominent, respected members of their communities. Their children are becoming doctors, lawyers, engineers, and corporate executives. They are proof positive that the American dream still works—if a person is willing to work hard. What makes the difference for these people? It all starts at home with parents who encourage and exhort their children to strive for success.

We certainly do understand how hard it can be to maintain an encouraging attitude. Let's face it, children do stupid and annoying things sometimes. A few days ago, a family down the street had made an appointment with a photographer to get a family portrait done. On the day they were supposed to get their picture taken, their four-year-old decided he needed a haircut in order to look his best. He also decided he could give himself a haircut—with his daddy's electric razor. As you might expect, the appointment with the photographer had to be rescheduled. Little Brucie looked like a puppy with a bad case of the mange.

When situations like that arise—or even when your children are a little too wound up at the end of a hard day—it's easy to get frustrated and angry and to say things that tear down rather than build up. That's why we urge you to pray, as we do, that God will help you be constructive, never destructive, in every situation that arises with your children.

Hard Work Can Be Fun

In his book *20 Things I Want My Kids to Know*, writer Hal Urban says, "Believe it or not, work is the preference of the healthy mind and body. The happiest people in this world are the most productive. Armand Hammer, the industrialist who died in 1990 at the age of ninety-two, was once asked how a man his age had the energy to continually circle the globe to conduct business. He said: 'I love my work. I can't wait to start a new day. I never wake up without being full of ideas. Everything is a challenge.' "

We believe that work is a gift from God, and we've tried to teach our children that this is the case. The Bible tells us that when God created the first man, Adam, he immediately gave him a job. Genesis 2:15 says, "The LORD God took the man and put him in the Garden of Eden to work it and take care of it." Adam was in paradise. And he was working.

Sadly, in modern American society, most people seem to think of work as a burden rather than a blessing. We often hear people talk about how much they hate Mondays and how much they look forward to Fridays. But by Sunday morning (or in some cases, Saturday evening), they're already brooding about the fact that Monday is coming. Life isn't supposed to be that way! If a person hates the work he does, that usually means he chose the wrong career. Yes, there are other variables that can make the workplace unpleasant. A critical, unappreciative boss can ruin anyone's day. So can unfriendly coworkers or difficult working conditions or an insufficient salary. But these are, for the most part, temporary conditions that can be solved by finding a better job.

We've always believed that when it comes to work, if you don't like what you're doing, you ought to find something else to do. Now, it is a tragic mistake to think that your work can bring you all the personal satisfaction and pleasure you need. But it's just as big a mistake to think of work as a necessary evil.

So it is important to help our children develop a proper attitude about work. Their futures may very well depend upon it. There's an interesting quote in the best-selling little business book *FISH!*, an allegory about Seattle's world-famous fishmarket, Pike Place Market. Mary Jane, the central personality in the book, wrote, "There is always a choice about the way you do your work, even if there is not a choice about the work itself." And as Ralph Waldo Emerson said, "People are compensated according to the value of their contributions." If you want to get more out of life, you have to put more into life. If you want to be successful, you have to work hard—whether you're an adult working for a corporation, a high-school student studying geometry, or a child playing T-ball.

Derek Jeter, a perennial all-star shortstop with the New York Yankees, remembers that he began playing baseball when he was four and his grandmother would put a ball on a tee for him. After that, Derek would spend many hours on the baseball diamond sharpening his skills. His mother says, "My husband always told Derek to compare himself with kids who really wanted to play ball." In other words, don't settle for anything less than striving to be the best of the best.

And Derek didn't "settle" in sports or in academics. When Derek was a boy, his father had him and his sister, Sharlee, sign a contract at the beginning of every school term, spelling out what was expected of them that year. Their father explained, "We wanted them to do well academically. And we wanted them to be involved in things. The contract spelled out study hours, curfews, and participation in school activities."

"We told him if he worked hard, he'd have options," Derek's mother said. And she was right.

In high school Derek starred in basketball and baseball, was selected to the National Honor Society, and served as president of the Latin Club. He says now, "I always wanted to be one of the best. My mom said I could be if I kept working. I guess she was right."

You may be saying, "But we can't all be as successful as Derek Jeter." Our answer to that is, "Why not?" Actress/singer Jennifer Lopez is another who credits her success to her parents' urging her to work hard: "It constantly amazes me that somebody like me could be doing the stuff that I'm doing," she says. "I knew I could because my mom always told me that if you work hard, then you can achieve anything."

Motivational speaker/author Brian Tracy says that many studies have been conducted over the years in an attempt to determine why some people are more successful than others. He writes, "Hundreds, and even thousands of salespeople, staff and managers have been interviewed, tested, and studied in an attempt to identify the common denominators of success. One of the most important success factors discovered, over and over again, is the quality of 'action orientation.'"

In other words, people who are successful don't just dream about being successful. They work hard to become successful. They don't wait for life to come to them. They go after life! Tracy says:

Successful people are intensely action oriented. They seem to move faster than unsuccessful people. They are busier. They try more and try harder. They start a little earlier and they stay a little later. They are in constant motion.

Unsuccessful people, on the other hand, start at the last moment necessary and quit at the first moment possible. They're fastidious about taking every minute of coffee breaks, lunch hours, sick leave, and vacations. They sometimes brag, "When I am at work, I never even think about it."

Tracy goes on to tell of a survey of self-made millionaires—that is, men and women who did not inherit their fortunes, but who built them from the ground up. He says that these successful people "almost unanimously agreed that their success was the result of always doing more than they were paid for."

We parents need to teach our children that there are rewards to be gained from doing more than we require of them. Most schoolteachers allow their students to turn in extra-credit assignments to improve their grades, and we parents ought to follow their example. There are plenty of chores to do around the house. Wouldn't it be great if your children were looking for ways they could help you instead of waiting for you to tell them what to do? They might just do that if they knew they were going to be rewarded for their efforts.

Bottom line: It's important to teach our kids that hard work pays off and that you usually get out of life only what you put into it. To be a true winner in life, you must work hard. To have a true sense of self-worth, you must contribute to something or someone other than yourself. Life isn't always easy, but it can always be fun if you are involved in work that you love.

We love what we do. We look forward to getting up each morning because we know that each day will be a challenge. It will provide us with an opportunity to contribute something worthwhile to our children as well as to others we come in contact with—people in the sports world and in corporate America. We want our children to experience that same joy of accomplishment, so we encourage them to find something—anything—they love to do and then to work hard doing it.

If they do, life will always be fun, interesting, exciting, and fulfilling!

PART SIX

An Extra Helping
of Blessings for Parents

Chapter 15

For Mothers Only

No man is poor who has a godly mother.
Abraham Lincoln

S orry, guys, but this chapter is for the moms among us. I (Ruth) want to take a few moments to talk to moms about their vital role in their children's healthy growth and development. Dads, if you want to come along, that's great because you just might learn a few things. But I want to warn you in advance that there's not going to be anything about sports in this chapter!

Instead here's a story most mothers can relate to: The *Miami Herald* reports that Michelle Tribout's children drove her up a tree—literally. This mother of three children, including two teenagers, climbed a tree in her family's backyard and refused to come down until her family let her know that they appreciate everything she does for them. Before climbing the tree and taking up residence in her kids' tree house, Mrs. Tribout had posted a sign in front of her home, reading: On Strike Mom! No Cooking, Cleaning, Doctoring, Banking, or Taxi Service. Out of Order.

She told a reporter, "I wait on them hand and foot. I love them. I'd do anything in the world for them, but they're going to treat me nice."

After spending one night in the tree house, she came down. Her children—Misty, fifteen, Joseph, thirteen, and Rachel, seven, had done some chores and baked her some brownies. Her husband told the newspaper that he understood what drove his wife to go on strike: "Two teens in the house." (Ha! He should try sixteen of them!)

Do *you* understand how Michelle Tribout felt? You do if you've been a mother for any length of time! It can be frustrating to be a mother—especially in our society, where it sometimes seems as if moms get all of the blame and none of the credit. Flip through a half-dozen television channels on a typical afternoon, and you're likely to see at least a couple of misfits on talk shows blaming their mothers for their pathetic condition. Often Mom bears the brunt of jokes on sitcoms, in movies, comic strips, and commercials, and by stand-up comedians. We moms can be tempted to borrow Rodney Dangerfield's old line: "I don't get no respect."

But you know what? The view I've been describing is a very distorted one. In fact, it's a lie. So throughout the rest of this chapter, I'm going to give you some very important truths about motherhood.

MOTHERS ARE THE MOST RESPECTED, MOST LOVED, MOST LISTENED TO, AND MOST INFLUENTIAL PEOPLE IN THE WORLD

Motherhood is the highest calling any woman could answer, and it brings tremendous rewards. Consider that six hundred college students were asked to write down their favorite word, and 422 of them turned in the same one. That's right: *Mother.*

In his book *Traveling Light for Mothers,* Max Lucado tells of a similar survey undertaken by Doremus Advertising Company. A number of CEOs were asked which family member had been most inspirational to them personally and most influential in their career. Sixty-four percent said that person was Mom.

We mothers have incredible power and influence. It's up to us to use it wisely, and that's not always easy to do, especially in the middle of a hectic ninety-eight-miles-per-hour day when everybody wants your attention and nobody seems to notice that you only have two hands.

Chuck Swindoll issues this challenge, "A harmonious marital partnership and a solid, unselfish commitment to motherhood have never been of greater importance to you or, for that matter, to our nation. Talk about a challenge worth your effort." He goes on to echo some of what I've already said. "In spite of what you may have heard, this role is the most dignified, the most influential, and the most rewarding in all the world." He also says that there is no other influence in the world so great as a mother: "Their words are never fully forgotten, their touch leaves an indelible impression, and the memory of their presence lasts a lifetime."

God Has Chosen Mothers to Be His Hands and Feet, Ministering His Love to Our Children

Jesus even compared his love to that of a mother. As he lamented over Jerusalem, he said, "How often I have longed to gather your children together, as a hen gathers her chicks under her wings, but you were not willing" (Matthew 23:37).

And speaking through the prophet, God asks, "Can a mother forget the baby at her breast and have no compassion for the child she has borne? Though she may forget, I will not forget you!" (Isaiah 49:15).

Being a loving, caring mother to her children is one of the most godly things a woman can do. That's why I strive to remember these words penned by Amy Nappa in her book, *A Woman's Touch:*

> Because of the vast amount of time we'll spend with our children during their lives, they're probably the ones who will be the most influenced, changed and molded by our touch. So, touch carefully! Pour honey into their hearts instead of vinegar. Give them your best side instead of your worst. Bring out the company dishes for them. Write them notes to remind them of your love.... Speak gently to them. Remember, the lips that kiss their wounds can also lay open new heartaches. Compliment them on their strengths and encourage them in their weaknesses. The best tribute your children can give you is to grow up to be wise and loving men and women who follow Jesus. Be intentional in touching them. Show them the grace and love God has shown you. They're your legacy to a world that desperately needs His touch.

In a way, I see the role of a mother as being like that of John the Baptist. When John's disciples came to him and complained that Jesus was drawing the crowds to himself, John said, "He must become greater; I must become less" (John 3:30). Our role is to help our children grow stronger so that we can eventually watch them fly from the nest. One of the ways we can do this is to help them learn to lean more on God and less on us.

Because we mothers are given the responsibility and the privilege of representing God to our children, we must strive to be godly people. I believe there is no better description of a godly wife and mother than the one found in Proverbs 31:10-31:

> A wife of a noble character who can find?
>   She is worth far more than rubies.
> Her husband has full confidence in her
>   and lacks nothing of value.
> She brings him good, not harm,
>   all the days of her life.
> She selects wool and flax
>   and works with eager hands.
> She is like the merchant ships,
>   bringing her food from afar.
> She gets up while it is still dark;
>   she provides food for her family
>   and portions for her servant girls.
> She considers a field and buys it;
>   out of her earnings she plants a vineyard.
> She sets about her work vigorously;
>   her arms are strong for her tasks.
> She sees that her trading is profitable,
>   and her lamp does not go out at night.
> In her hand she holds the distaff
>   and grasps the spindle with her fingers.

She opens her arms to the poor
>and extends her hands to the needy.

When it snows, she has no fear for her household;
>for all of them are clothed in scarlet.

She makes coverings for her bed;
>she is clothed in fine linen and purple.

Her husband is respected at the city gate,
>where he takes his seat among the elders of the land.

She makes linen garments and sells them,
>and supplies the merchants with sashes.

She is clothed with strength and dignity;
>she can laugh at the days to come.

She speaks with wisdom,
>and faithful instruction is on her tongue.

She watches over the affairs of her household
>and does not eat the bread of idleness.

Her children arise and call her blessed;
>her husband also, and he praises her:

Many women do noble things,
>but you surpass them all.

Charm is deceptive, and beauty is fleeting;
>but a woman who fears the LORD is to be praised.

Give her the reward she has earned,
>and let her works bring her praise at the city gate.

Wow! Sounds like a very tall order, doesn't it? But if we go back through that passage, we will find that there are thirteen hallmarks of such a godly wife and mother:

1. She is a loving partner to her husband (verses 11-12).
2. She is trustworthy and reliable (verse 11).
3. She looks out for the welfare of others (verses 12,15).
4. She works hard (verses 13-15,27).

5. She sees to it that her family's needs are met (verses 15,18, 21,27).
6. She handles money wisely (verse 16).
7. She is smart (verses 16,27).
8. She is a person of great inner strength (verse 26).
9. She is generous and kind (verse 20).
10. She is dignified (verse 25).
11. She is wise and gives good advice (verse 26).
12. She has a sense of humor and does not worry about the future (verse 25).
13. She has a proper relationship with God (verse 30).

These are qualities that any woman who really wants them can develop. No one is just naturally a terrific mother. Oh, some women naturally have more patience than other women. Some people naturally have a great sense of humor. Others are naturally intelligent or have a knack for stretching a dollar. Some mothers are strong in areas where you are weak, and you are strong in areas where other mothers are weak. No one will have all of the thirteen qualities listed above in equal amounts. But all of us can work on improving ourselves in those areas where we are lacking; we can all become great mothers.

But don't shoot for perfection. That's an impossible goal. Nobody is perfect. Anyone who won't settle for anything less than perfection is going to be constantly frustrated and disappointed. But as Ruth Graham said, "If I cannot give my children a perfect mother, I can at least give them more of the one they've got—and make that one more loving. I will be available. I will take time to listen, time to play, time to be home when they arrive from school, time to counsel and encourage."

It certainly wasn't easy for me to go from being a single mother of one child to being a married mother of nineteen. Many situations arose that I had never encountered before. I was driven to my knees, and with God's help I grew stronger and more capable.

It's an awesome responsibility and a tremendous privilege to be a mother. It can be overwhelming and even terrifying. But you can do it! You *can* be a great mother! And as Alfred Armand Montapert said: "There was never a great man or woman who did not have a great mother. At the mother's knee, around the home fireside, the foundations of life are laid. Great persons are great because of good, strong foundations on which they were able to build a character."

A Mother's Hard Work Does Pay Off

It's true—even though you may not think so right now.

As far as I'm concerned, the human mother is a creature who disproves the theory of evolution. If our bodies were able to adapt to the demands of our environment, we would be radically different. For example, we'd have ten hands so we could handle all the needs of those who count on us. We'd have eyes in the back of our heads so we could see what our kids were up to at all times. (Better yet, we'd be equipped with a radar system that keeps track of every move our children make.) We'd have multiple heads so we could wear all of our hats at the same time—chef's hat, nurse's hat, teacher's hat, chauffeur's hat, policeman's hat, referee's hat, housekeeper's hat, and the list goes on. And we'd have electronic schedulers built into our brains so we could keep track of everyone's routines, doctor's appointments, clothing needs, school assignments, and so on.

But we moms are making do with just two hands, two eyes, and so forth. Even so, I agree with Lisa Auther that "any mother could perform the jobs of several air-traffic controllers with ease." But I guarantee all that hustle and bustle will produce results whether or not you can see it now.

Sometimes seeing the rewards of mothering can be like seeing the growth of a bamboo tree. It doesn't grow an inch for the first five years after it's planted, but then it shoots up nearly one hundred feet during the sixth year. Just when you're thinking your children have never heard a single word you've said, they'll surprise you by showing that they really *have* been paying attention.

In the meantime, hang on and try to keep smiling. As we said earlier, it really helps to have a healthy sense of humor. For example, Shirley Ratcliff writes: "When our daughter Kathy was participating in a parenting class at her church, she explained to her six-year-old daughter, Kayla, that she was taking a course to help make her a better mommy. The next Sunday after church, Kayla became upset and threw a tantrum because she was not getting her way. Both parents tried to calm her. But with tears streaming down her face, Kayla announced loudly to her mother, 'You told me you were taking a course to make you a better mommy. Well, it's not working!' "

Oh yes! There will be moments like this. Possibly many of them! But these too shall pass. As someone wise once said, "If it were going to be easy to raise kids, it never would have started with something called labor."

As I write these words, I have a number of Mother's Day cards spread out before me, treasures that I have saved in my memory box. When I look at the inscriptions on these cards, I know that I wouldn't trade being a mother for anything else in the world.

Before I share these notes with you, I want to say that I do so cautiously and with great humility. I've never shared them with anyone before. Until now I've kept them in a little leopard-skin keepsake box. Then, whenever I'm facing a big problem with one of our kids, I open that little box, take the cards out, and read them again. They boost my spirits and remind me that even the worst situations can be resolved.

The cards also serve to remind me that even if children say they hate you and desert you, most of them will eventually come back to the right path. We mothers need to know that our children will eventually realize that we sometimes had to do and say things that were hard for them precisely because we love them. During my difficult parenting times, these cards give me comfort and help me rejoice—even when it seems there's no reason to rejoice.

For example, one card says, *Terrific moms like you…are angels in disguise. Love you. Happy Mom's Day.* Inside Caroline has written, *Mom, I couldn't be more thankful for what you have done for me. I hope Mother's Day is as special as you are. I love you.* Suddenly, I forget about our battle over the cut blanket and her six months of being grounded. All I can see is the beautiful young woman she has become.

Another, from Stephen, reads: *Words can't express how great you are.*

I'm getting a little bit misty as I read these words from Dani: *You are a wonderful mother and a wonderful person. Thanks for everything!*

From Stephanie: *You are the greatest! Thanks for being you. I love you.*

Daughter Karyn and her husband, Dale, wrote, *Thank you for being such a great mom to both of us.*

From David: *There are so many things I want to say to you. I just want to let you know that you are exactly what a perfect mother is. Yes, a perfect mother! Your love for all of us is incredible. You really make me feel loved when I'm around you. God does answer prayers when you ask for a special person in your life. I love you. David.* (This message is especially meaningful to me because David was in Iraq from March to August of 2003. He returned, and we're very glad he's safe.)

From Brian: *You're the greatest person I've ever known. Thanks for everything you do for me. Love, Brian.*

Sammy writes, *Maybe it's that I've grown a little, but regardless, I'm appreciating you more every day. I love you, and thank you for being just the way you are.*

I could go on, but I won't. I'll just say that I know there were times when these kids didn't think I was the greatest and when they weren't exactly thankful for me. That's because I had to get tough with them from time to time. But over the years, as they've matured in their perspective, our kids have come to realize that when I was tough, or when I had to say no, I wasn't doing it *to* them, but rather *for* them, to help them become the adults they are capable of being.

Give your kids time to grow up. You may not feel as if your children appreciate you now, but they will. You may not think they are listening to you now, but they are. All of your hard work will pay off! As Marion C. Garretty said, "Mother love is the fuel that enables a normal human being to do the impossible."

YES, WE CAN CHANGE THE WORLD!

I'm sure you've heard this quote from William Ross Wallace: "The hand that rocks the cradle rules the world." Well, it's true! Consider this: In the early 1800s the world's attention was focused on Napoleon Bonaparte's triumphant march through Europe. But while Napoleon was heading toward Waterloo, some very important babies were being born:

- Britain's future prime minister **William Gladstone** was born in Liverpool.
- **Abraham Lincoln** came into the world in Kentucky.
- The poet **Alfred Lord Tennyson** also drew his first breath, as did **Oliver Wendell Holmes** and composer **Felix Mendelssohn.**

Any intelligent observer would have thought that Napoleon was changing the world during that year of 1809. He wasn't. Instead, the world was being changed by the mothers of the babies who were born that year. Because of the nurturing care their mothers provided, those men grew up to lead their nations, to liberate men from captivity, and to transform society through the poetry, music, and literature they gave us. As Napoleon himself said, "The future destiny of a child is always the work of the mother."

Supporting that assertion are a number of American presidents who have admitted they were "mama's boys" and that their mother's support and belief in them had helped them achieve positions of leadership. James Garfield, for example, credited his success to his mother's "blind confidence." As he lay dying after being shot by an assassin, he reportedly found comfort by writing a letter to his beloved mother. Woodrow Wilson said he came to appreciate the strength of womanhood through "the apron strings" of his mother. According to writer Tim Elmore, Teddy Roosevelt considered himself to be "a carbon copy" of his mom, and "Franklin D. Roosevelt wouldn't even dare go to school without his mother, and that school was Harvard University!" Elmore writes, "She went with him, organizing his life, as he attended college. While he was an extreme case, he again represents the drive and the wings a man can receive from a parent. She almost pushed him into greatness."

Here is a small sampling of what other great men and women have said about the importance of mothers.

- **George Washington:** "Mothers work, not upon canvas that shall perish, nor marble that crumbles into dust, but upon mind, upon spirit,

which is to last forever and which is to bear, for good or evil, throughout its duration, the impress of a mother's hand."

- **Wilma Rudolph** (Oops! I guess I lied about no sports in this chapter! Wilma recovered from a childhood battle with polio to become
  an Olympic champion runner.): "The doctors told me I would never
  walk, but my mother told me I would...so I believed my mother."
- **Artist Marc Chagall:** "My mother's love for me was so great that
  I have worked hard to justify it."
- **Heavyweight boxing champion Joe Louis:** "I hope they're still making women like my mama. She always told me to do the right thing.
  She always told me to have pride in myself; she said a good name is
  better than money."
- **Thomas Edison:** "I did not have my mother long, but she cast over
  me an influence that has lasted all my life.... Her firmness, her sweet-
  ness, her goodness, were potent powers to keep me on the right path.
  My mother was the making of me. The memory of her will always be
  a blessing to me."
- **Dr. Benjamin Spock:** "I really learned it all from my mother."
- **Pope Paul VI:** "Every mother is like Moses. She prepares a world she
  will not see."

More Than Anything Else, It Is the Mother Who Makes the Home

There is nothing more comforting to a child than to know that his mother loves
him. If his mother is there, a shack can be the most wonderful place on earth.

A friend of mine tells of seeing the house where he grew up for the first
time in about twenty years. He was surprised to discover how small the house
really was. The "huge" yard where he had spent so many hours playing Wiffle
Ball with his friends was only slightly bigger than a postage stamp. The neighborhood itself wasn't anything to brag about, and the house that he remembered so fondly was the poorest in the neighborhood.

Then it occurred to him that the house itself had never been that special. It was the love and security provided by the presence of his mother that had transformed this old house into the happiest place a little boy had ever known. J. R. Bookhoff is right on target: "It's the atmosphere created by the mother that makes the home worthwhile."

Motherhood Is Not a Science

Momhood is more of an art than a science. It's not like math, where two plus two always equals four. It's more like psychology than internal medicine. In other words, what works great for one mom may not work the same way for the next one. There's ample room in this business for trial and error, for keeping at it until you find out what works best for you.

Don't think you have to approach every situation the way James Dobson tells you to. Kevin Leman doesn't have all the answers you need. Neither does Dr. Spock or Dr. Laura or Pat and Ruth Williams. Although it's true that certain principles work better than others, nobody has all the answers you need. Remember instead that there really is something powerful about a mother's instinct.

Because mothering is the sort of thing we learn as we go along, please don't be afraid to ask for help when you need it. Barbara Schiller, writing in *Christian Parenting Today*, says, "So many of us believe we can make the parenting journey on our own. Leaning on someone else or asking for advice feels like failure, but…when we trust one another with our burdens…we allow God to touch us through our friends. We allow them to be bearers of His care and comfort." She says, "It takes courage to ask for help when we need it."

And we all need help.

Allison Pearson, author of *I Don't Know How She Does It*, tells the following story in *Time Magazine:*

A mother in Boston was feeling guilty, as mothers do. Her daughter had told her that she was the only mom who never took her kid to

Brownies. Now that probably wasn't true, but it is the child's role to make the mother feel bad about things she hasn't done enough, as well as things she simply hasn't done. So the day of the next Brownie meeting, Mom got to the office early, rushed through her tasks, then made an excuse and left. She drove across town like Sandra Bullock in *Speed*. Arriving at the Brownie meeting, Mom sat down and basked for a few moments in a glow of satisfaction. It was then that she noticed the Brownie leader looking at her: "It's lovely to see you, Mrs. Johnson," the woman said. "But maybe next time you could bring your daughter as well." "I forgot the kid," the mom recalls. "Can you believe it, I forgot the kid!"

Don't feel bad if you blow it sometimes. Mothers are heroic. They're indispensable. They're the heart and soul of their families. But still, beneath it all, we're only human beings!

Chapter 16

FOR FATHERS ONLY

Fatherhood must be at the core of the universe.

C. S. LEWIS

This is Pat, with a few words for dads.

I am sometimes amazed when I consider my tender feelings for my children. There were times, especially when my kids were younger, when I would wake up in the middle of the night and be seized with the desire to get out of bed and go tiptoe into all of their rooms just to make sure they were okay. I wanted to tell them I loved them even if they couldn't hear me.

Have my children disobeyed me? Yes.

Have my children made a mess of things and left it for me to clean up? Yes.

Whatever your children might do that makes you angry, sad, or disappointed, I've been there. But I also know the joy a father feels when one of his children comes up, wraps her arms around him, and says, "Daddy, I love you!"

As we've said before in this book, the most important thing any father can do for a child is to help him develop a right relationship with God through faith in Christ. However, there are other important things I hope you learn from reading this book:

YOUR CHILDREN NEED YOU

- They need you to show them that a father's heart can be tender and kind.

- They need you to tell them often how much you love them and that you always will.
- They need you to be gentle with them even in situations where you must also be firm.
- They need you to show your love for their mother, so they will feel secure.
- They need to know that you love them even when they don't live up to your expectations and that you will be the first to forgive them when they need it.
- They need you to teach them things about life: how to fly a kite, how to tie a tie, how to treat other people, and how to grow into the people they were always meant to be.

My dad left a huge imprint on my life. He was born and raised in Greensboro, North Carolina, educated at the University of North Carolina, went to Philadelphia to teach school, and taught a Sunday school class at Bryn Mawr Presbyterian Church. There he met my mother.

I was the only son of four children, and my dad was crazy about me. He was my biggest cheerleader and, next to my mother, my biggest fan. He played catch with me in our side yard. He took me to my first big league baseball game in Philadelphia when I was seven, and that started my lifelong interest in sports. He was always there for me, and he helped me grow into the person I am today.

My dad was an active member in the community of Wilmington, Delaware, where I grew up. He was into everything.

Dad was killed in an automobile accident returning from my college graduation at Wake Forest University in 1962. I was twenty-two years old. I never really knew him as an adult, but I think we'd have enjoyed each other and become good friends.

I did, however, have another father role-model growing up. My best friend was Ruly Carpenter, and his dad, Bob, owned the Phillies. Bob played ball with all of us kids. He threw batting practice at the field in their yard and took us to the ballpark in Philadelphia on a regular basis. We also went to the

Phillies' spring training site in Clearwater, Florida, every March while we were in high school. To this day, I can still hear Bob Carpenter's voice hollering at us, teasing us, cheering for us. It's been well over forty years ago, but the memory is still alive to me.

These two fathers invested their time and energy in Ruly and me, and it made a big difference in how we turned out.

Your Children Need Encouragement, Not Abuse

Few things make me as angry as a father who is abusive to his children.

Because I have been active in sports all my life, I have seen more than my fair share of abusive fathers. Now don't get me wrong. I love sports. I believe that participating in athletics helps kids develop in many important ways. Sports teaches the importance of teamwork, hard work, and sportsmanship. Participating in athletic events teaches kids how to win graciously and how to lose without losing your self-respect. And sports teaches that it is possible to bounce back from failure and succeed.

But too many fathers forget that more is going on in sports than just winning on the field. I've heard fathers berate their boys for striking out in Little League. I've heard insulting remarks directed at kids because they fumbled the ball or dropped a catchable pass in a peewee football game. I've seen fathers become absolutely livid because their child "embarrassed" them by her sloppy play in a soccer game.

Now I expect my kids to try hard out there. I expect them to do their best and to learn from their mistakes. But this kind of encouraging is vastly different from abusing kids. When I hear dads yelling at their children because of some mistake made on the athletic field, I have to wonder what goes on at home. How many boys and girls suffer constantly from having fathers who are angry, sarcastic, and impossible to please?

Dads, we have to remember that children have fragile egos and tender hearts which are easily damaged. I think that we dads are especially tough on our boys. We want them to act like little soldiers and be tough. But they're not soldiers. They're children! They need nurturing. According to a twenty-eight-year study conducted by Emory University, "High-achieving boys had very nurturing fathers for the first ten years of life—cuddling and rocking them to sleep as infants or comforting them when they were afraid of the dark." Psychologist John Snarey told *USA Today* that early nurturing from their fathers may give boys a "nontraditional" edge of security that vaults them ahead in life. The study also found that high-achieving girls "had dads who supported athletic training and were emotionally close to them during the teen years— teaching them to drive, taking them to karate lessons or on camping trips."

I know that one of the reasons you are reading this book is to learn from the experiences Ruth and I have had as parents. Well, Ruth and I have greatly benefited from the experiences of other parents who were willing to share their experiences. For example, I learned from one father who said:

My family's all grown and the kids are all gone. But if I had it to do over, this is what I'd do:

- I would love my wife more in front of my children.
- I would laugh with my children more—at our mistakes and our joys.
- I would listen more, even to the littlest child.
- I would be more honest about my own imperfections, never pretending perfection.
- I would pray differently for my family. Instead of focusing on their shortcomings, I'd focus on mine.
- I would do more things with my children.
- I would encourage them more and bestow more praise.
- I would pay more attention to little things, like thoughtful deeds and words.
- I would share God more intimately with my family. Every ordinary thing that happened in every ordinary day I would use to direct them to God.

I've also learned from men like Thomas Edison, who was a terrific inventor, but a not-so-terrific father. His namesake, Thomas Edison Jr., once wrote to a friend, "I probably will never be able to please him. I have no genius, no talent, and no accomplishment. I'm afraid it's not in me."

When another son, William, wrote letters home from boarding school, his father returned them with all of his spelling errors corrected, and a note that said: *Wm.—see marks—your spelling makes me faint.*

Not exactly the sort of encouragement a child needs from his father.

YOUR CHILDREN NEED A LIVE-IN DAD

Sigmund Freud said, "I cannot think of any need, in childhood, as strong as the need for a father's protection." Sadly, more children than ever before are growing up without that protection. Often, Dad walked out when things got tough. Sometimes when there was difficulty in the marriage, Dad decided, *To heck with this. I'd rather be single.* Sometimes Dad met someone at work who was prettier, funnier, or more attentive than his children's mom. And to be fair, sometimes Mom decided that she wasn't happy in the marriage and left the family.

It is totally beyond my comprehension how any father (or mother) could turn his back on his own children. And yet the number of American children growing up in homes without a father has quadrupled since 1950, leaving millions of children in families headed by a woman. The Annie E. Casey Foundation reports that nineteen million children—just fewer than 25 percent of all the children in the United States—were living in homes without fathers in 1994. In 1950 only 6 percent of America's children were living in homes where there was no father.

Douglas Nelson, executive director of the foundation, said, "This is a dramatic demographic trend." He went on to explain that children who grow up in homes without fathers are five times more likely to be poor, twice as likely to drop out of high school, and far more likely to end up in foster care or juvenile justice facilities.

This situation is so troubling that even noted feminist Gloria Steinem said, "Most American children suffer too much mother and too little father."

As author Sara Gilbert said, "It may be hard on some fathers not to have a son, but it is much harder on a boy not to have a father."

Evangelist Bill Glass put it this way: "Today's teens are the victims of the fatherless generation."

And yet, as James Dobson writes, "If American families are to survive the incredible stresses and dangers they now face, it will be because husbands and fathers provide loving leadership in their homes and rank their wives and children at the highest level on their system of priorities."

YOUR CHILDREN NEED BRIDGE-BUILDERS

In chapter 15, Ruth quoted Pope Paul VI, who said that all mothers are like Moses, in that they are preparing a world they will never see. He was referring to the fact that Moses led the children of Israel out of Egypt and served as their leader for forty years, but he was never allowed to enter the Promised Land.

In the same way, mothers and fathers prepare their children for the life they will live in this world after we have gone home to be with the Lord. We are building bridges so that our children can cross over to a land we will never visit.

YOUR CHILDREN NEED YOUR UNDERSTANDING

Take it from me, there's going to come a time when you are an embarrassment to your children—and it may come quicker than you think! It's not easy when you reach the point where the child who once thought you were Abraham Lincoln, George Washington, Superman, and the Incredible Hulk all rolled into one suddenly comes to think of you as a cross between Captain Kangaroo and Goofy. But one cardinal rule of parenting is "no hurt feelings." Just know that this phase is going to happen, it will last anywhere from a few months to a few years, and then it will pass.

A woman reported that she sat at singer Billy Joel's table during a charity fund-raiser. Joel's twelve-year-old daughter was seated at the same table. Just before the singer was introduced, his daughter gave him a withering look and pleaded, "Please don't sing, Daddy. It's soooo embarrassing!"

Did my father ever embarrass me? You bet. He was a warm, outgoing man who never met a stranger. He came to all my baseball games and yelled enthusiastically—sometimes too enthusiastically. In fact sometimes I'd tell him to go to the wrong field because I was so embarrassed.

When I was a freshman at Wake Forest, Dad would still attend some of the games even though I wasn't playing on the varsity team. During one game at the University of Maryland, the Good Humor ice cream truck went by, and my dad bought popsicles for every player on the team, took them into the dugout, and handed them out. I was definitely embarrassed when I heard what had happened. The guys on the varsity team really let me have it, even though they enjoyed their popsicles on that hot, sunny day. As I look back now, I smile inside. As a dad myself, I know what my dad was doing. He wanted to show his support.

The late advice columnist Ann Landers drew up this chronological view of the way children see their fathers:

- *At four years old:* "My daddy can do anything."
- *At five:* "My daddy knows a whole lot."
- *At six:* "My dad is smarter than your dad."
- *At eight:* "My dad doesn't exactly know *everything*."
- *At ten:* "In the olden days, when my dad grew up, things were sure different."
- *At twelve:* "Oh, well, naturally Dad doesn't know anything about that. He's too old to remember his childhood."
- *At fourteen:* "Don't pay any attention to my dad. He's so old-fashioned."
- *At twenty-one:* "Dad is hopelessly out of date."
- *At twenty-five:* "Dad knows about it, but he should because he's been around so long."

- *At thirty:* "Maybe we should ask my dad what he thinks. After all he's had a lot of experience."
- *At forty:* "I wonder how my dad would have handled it. He was so wise."
- *At fifty:* "I'd give anything if Dad were here now so I could talk this over with him. Too bad I didn't appreciate how smart he was. I could have learned a lot from him."

Have my children been embarrassed by me? Oh, you bet they have! They're very normal in that regard. But it passed. In fact, here are some of the notes those once-embarrassed children wrote me in a single twelve-month period:

- Dani: *I know I say this a lot, but I feel like the luckiest girl in the world to have you for a dad! You mean everything to me. I love you more than words can express.*
- Sarah: *I love you so much. Thank you for supporting me in my decision to go back to school.*
- Andrea: *Your support in my new endeavors means the world to me.*
- Brian: *Thank you for everything you have done for me. It has been a long journey, but I hope we have many more Father's Days together.*
- Karyn: *Thanks, Dad, for everything you have done for me. I couldn't ask for anything more. You are the best dad anyone could have. You are the inspiration in my life.*
- Kati: *Thank you for adopting me. I enjoy living in the United States of America. Thank you for everything you have done for me. I love you very much, Dad!*

On Father's Day 2003, we received a message from David. He was calling from Iraq to talk to me. We were at church and missed his call, but here's what his message said: "Dad, we had a basketball tournament today, and our team won. Our prize was the opportunity to call home. I just wanted to tell you I love you. You're always saying I'm your hero, but Dad, I just wanted you to know that you're my hero. Thanks for all you've done for me. I can't wait to get home to see you. It's been quite an experience, and I can't wait to talk to you."

So hang in there during the difficult times. As hard as this may be for you (and for all dads), your children's embarrassment and the difficult times they give you are simply a means God uses to help your children grow, wean themselves away from total dependence on you, and prepare to build a life of their own.

Imagine how Joseph and Mary must have felt when they took Jesus to the temple when he was twelve years old. The Bible tells us that they had already traveled for a day on their way back to Nazareth when they noticed their son was missing. It took three days of searching before they found him "in the temple courts, sitting among the teachers, listening to them and asking them questions."

Mary, who was quite naturally worried and upset, said to him, "Son, why have you treated us like this? Your father and I have been anxiously searching for you."

He replied, "Why were you searching for me? Didn't you know I had to be in my Father's house?" (Luke 2:41-49).

Does it sound just a little bit like Jesus was embarrassed by his parents' concern for him? Probably so. I doubt if there's ever been a parent who wasn't an embarrassment to his child at one time or other. As Charles Wadsworth wrote, "By the time a man realizes that maybe his father was right, he usually has a son who thinks he's wrong."

YOUR CHILDREN NEED YOU TO BE AN EFFECTIVE LEADER

I believe that God expects the father to be the leader in the home. And I believe that because it's what the Bible teaches. However, I should add quickly that Jesus made it clear that anyone who wants to be the leader of all must be the servant of all (see Matthew 20:26). A leader is not someone who sits around and gives orders, who expects others to wait on him. A leader is one who is charged with the awesome responsibility of making sure all of his children are headed in the right direction.

I agree wholeheartedly with David Moore, who writes that in addition to the blessings fatherhood brings, "comes the curse of a magnanimous responsibility to love, lead, and prepare them for life. We are charged, by God our Father, to give them the proper foundation on which they can build a future based on His principles. We don't have a choice in the matter. Whether we like it or not, we will be held accountable for how well we do the job."

Rosey Grier, who had a hall-of-fame football career with the Rams, decries the fact that many fathers are not taking the proper leadership role in their families. "Many men go the other way and let their wives bring up the family," he writes. "To build a family on the love of God is the greatest thing a man can do."

Here are some other thoughts on fatherhood that are very much worth hearing:

- From Steve Farrar in his book, *Point Man:* "It is my God-appointed task to ensure that my sons will be ready to lead a family. I must equip them to that end. Little boys are the hope of the next generation. They are the fathers of tomorrow."
- From Tim Kimmel in *Basic Training for a Few God Men:* "The office of father is a sacred trust. You want to assume that trust and carry it out to and for God's glory."
- And from Larry Burkett: "Most families drift for lack of a rudder— the father's leadership. If a family's most important need is a godly father, and it is, then this need is far more important than all the material possessions a parent can provide."

Your Children Need You to Understand That It's an Honor to Be a Parent

Congressman J. C. Watts has known fame as a star quarterback for the University of Oklahoma and as a Republican representative from his state. He says, "Being called 'Congressman' is a real honor, but it doesn't hold a candle to being called 'Dad.' I know that being a father has been the most challenging and rewarding job I have ever taken on, and the most important."

C. Everett Koop, who served as surgeon general during the Reagan administration, echoes that thought when he says, "Life affords no greater responsibility, no greater privilege, than the raising of the next generation."

The late Fred Rogers, television's "Mr. Rogers," once said, "When we choose to be parents, we accept another human being as part of ourselves, and a large part of our emotional selves will stay with that person as long as we live. From that time on, there will be another person on this earth whose orbit around us will affect us as surely as the moon affects the tides and affect us in some ways more deeply than anyone else can." He added, "Our children are extensions of ourselves in ways our parents are not, nor our brothers and sisters, nor our spouses."

YOUR CHILDREN NEED YOU!

Recently Ruth and I had dinner with nine of our children. It was just one of those impromptu things that occasionally happens with our family. A few kids just happened to drop by (around dinnertime, of course), and we invited them to dinner. Then they called a few more, and they called a few more, and before we knew it, we had to make reservations for fifteen, counting boyfriends and girlfriends. But we relish the opportunity to get together and catch up on life.

On the way home after dinner, Ruth said to me, "It was really fun watching you preside over your kingdom tonight." I agreed. I loved seeing the children together conversing as adults. But deep down what I really enjoyed was seeing the way life had hit some of them in the face. I like to call it "coming to grips with remedial reality."

Some of our kids have been hit really hard with remedial reality, but that's the way they will learn and grow into mature, capable adults. Walt Disney once said, "We all need a good failure while we're young to help prepare us for the rest of life." And just as my father was always there for me, I will always be there for my kids.

More than any other thing, the boys and girls who call you Dad need you to give yourself to them. And the best way you can do that is by spending time with them, as this story illustrates:

> One day a group of young adults got to talking about the greatest gifts they had ever received from their parents. An attorney told the others that his favorite gift was a small box that came from his father one Christmas. Inside the box was a note, saying: *This year I will give you 365 hours—one hour every day, after dinner. It's yours. We'll talk about what you want to talk about. We'll go where you want to go, play whatever you want to play. It will be your hour!*
>
> As the others listened quietly, the young man went on, "My dad not only kept his promise, but he renewed it every year."
>
> As the others nodded in agreement, he concluded, "It's the greatest gift I ever had in my life. I am the result of my father's time."

Your children need your time, Dad. They need to know that they're important enough to merit your undivided attention when they talk to you. Believe me! At my house there have been times of so much conversation I'm sure things couldn't have been any more confusing at the Tower of Babel. But even when I've been pulled in nineteen different directions at once, I've done my best to show each of my children how much I value him or her. I couldn't possibly give each of my children an hour every day because that would leave me five hours for everything else in life. Besides that, I spend hundreds of hours on the road every year. But when I'm home I make room for one-on-one time as often as I possibly can.

Recently, I came across the following anonymous poem:

Remembering the Little Things That Make Fathers Special

He carried you on his shoulders
when you were too tired to walk.
He tucked you in at night
and told you bedtime stories.

He showed you how to bait a fishing hook
and how to hit a baseball.
He built you castles in the sand
and igloos in the snow.
He explained your schoolwork
in a way you could understand.
He made pancakes for breakfast on Sunday mornings.
He gave you advice,
but supported your decisions.
He was the first to forgive you
when you made a mistake.

That's pretty much the way I want my children to remember me. How about you?

AFTERWORD

It's a rare quiet afternoon at the Williams house.

Our children's schedules have them scattering in different directions, and in a scheduling fluke that happens about once every blue moon, we have the evening off.

This manuscript sits on the kitchen counter, ready to be shipped to our publisher. And neither one of us wants to let it go. That's because we are filled with doubts. Have we said what we needed to say? Have we said too much? Have we talked too much about the heartaches involved with parenting, and not enough about the joys? Have we made it seem too hard or too easy? Have we come across as "preachy" when what we really want to do is simply to share the benefit of our hard-earned experience?

We both know that if we packed everything into this book that we both want to say, it would probably be twice as long as it is. We also know that there is a time when we have to say, "That's it," and put the manuscript in the mail. Ultimately, all we can do at this point is the same thing we do when one of our children leaves the nest: comfort ourselves with the knowledge that we have done our very best.

Our prayer is that you will find the contents of our book helpful, that you will be comforted by reading about some of our more difficult experiences, and that you will be encouraged and strengthened as a parent.

In our own walk as parents, we realize that we never would have made it this far without help from dozens of great people. We've had some wonderful nannies who've loved our kids and been loved by them in return. We've had terrific cooks and housekeepers.

We also think of all the outstanding teachers, coaches, Sunday-school leaders, and other wonderful people who have given our children a helping hand along the way. We'd also like to express our appreciation to the dozens of other parents who have helped out, shared in millions of miles of carpooling, and so on. We have had an amazing amount of assistance that made parenting nineteen children possible.

One of the most indispensable people in our world is Angel Garcia, our house manager. Angel does everything. He cuts the grass. He drives. He counsels. He fixes the plumbing. He maintains our cars. You name it, and he does it with a positive, helpful attitude. He is one of those selfless people you meet far too infrequently in life.

Recently Angel had quite an adventure that started with the simple task of taking out the trash. Now taking out the trash is no small matter, since, as you can imagine, a family as large as ours generates quite a bit of garbage. Anyway, Angel was taking the trash cans out to the curb when he heard something inside one of them. He looked down and saw a rodent's long, skinny tail sticking out from underneath a couple of plastic garbage bags.

A possum had climbed into one of the cans and was looking for his breakfast.

The possum discovered Angel at about the same time Angel discovered the possum. He popped up from the trash and looked Angel right in the eye. As he and the possum engaged each other in a staring contest, Angel carried the heavy trash can about two hundred yards, to the shores of Lake Killarney behind our house.

I (Pat) asked Angel later, "Were you scared?"

"No," he replied, "but the possum was."

Just before they reached the water's edge, the possum leaped out of the can, raced to the lake, jumped into the water, and began to swim away. Angel yelled after him, "I'm giving you one chance, buddy...but don't come back!"

As Angel headed back to the house, he saw something else unusual at the edge of the lake, an upturned mound of earth, a nest of some kind. He picked up a stick and poked it into the nest, and a deadly water moccasin raised its head out of the hole.

Angel rushed back to the house, where he grabbed an axe. Then he hurried back to the snake's nest and began digging it up. Inside were two adult snakes and six babies. One by one he pinned them down with his stick and cut their heads off with his axe.

Later, when I asked Angel how he knew how to handle the situation, he said, "Oh, I'm an old rattlesnake hunter from Texas."

Then I asked, "Why didn't some of the snakes try to escape while you were killing the other ones?"

"Oh, they won't do that," Angel said. "They're family. They stick together. One snake will never forsake the others."

Wow! Who would have thought that human beings could learn a lesson from some poisonous snakes!

But apparently we can.

Never forget that you are part of a family. That family includes you, your spouse, your children, and other relatives. It also includes other parents who are going through the same things you're going through.

Don't be shy about reaching out to others for help when you need it. Don't be shy about offering your help when you see that others need it. That's what family is all about.

And we urge you to remember that, as someone has said, "The course of your children's tomorrow depends upon what you put into their hearts today." Keep investing in your kids. Keep trusting God. And know that we are praying for your success.

And who knows? We may be back later with a few stories about grandparenting!

You can contact Pat Williams directly at:

Mr. Pat Williams
c/o Orlando Magic
8701 Maitland Summit Blvd.
Orlando, FL 32810
(407) 916-2404
pwilliams@orlandomagic.com

If you would like to set up a speaking engagement for Ruth or Pat Williams, please call or write Pat's assistant, Diana Basch, at the address above or call her at (407) 916-2454. Requests can also be faxed to (407) 916-2986 or e-mailed to dbasch@orlandomagic.com or ruthwilliamsfl@hotmail.com.

We would love to hear from you. Please send your comments about this book to Pat or Ruth Williams at the above address or in care of our publisher at the address below. Thank you.

c/o WaterBrook Press
2375 Telstar Drive, Suite 160
Colorado Springs, CO 80920
(719) 590-8977 fax

To learn more about WaterBrook Press and view
our catalog of products, log on to our Web site:
www.waterbrookpress.com

WATERBROOK
PRESS

Printed in the United States
by Baker & Taylor Publisher Services